The world of Aztecs

The world of Aztecs

by

William-H. Prescott

A Pierre Waleffe Book

Minerva

Contents

In this evocation of the Aztecs—by far the best—known people of ancient Mexico—the author mentions the various pre—Aztec civilizations of the country : for the reason we have thought it would be interesting to show, among the illustrations, some specimens of Toltec, Maya, and other, art or monuments.

Credits: Giraudon: pages 18, 26, 29, 38, 39a, 48, 80b, 83, 90, 92b, 95, 96, 98, 99, 107, 119, 120, 121, 122 - Pierre Vérité: 33 - Françoise Baudin: 46 - Roger Viollet: 2, 5, 7, 8, 9, 10, 11, 12, 15, 16, 17, 24, 27, 30, 31, 32, 34, 41, 42, 44, 51, 52, 54, 55, 57a, 60, 61, 62, 66, 69, 70, 74, 75, 78, 79, 81, 82a, b, 84, 87, 88, 93, 94, 100b, 101a, b, 104, 113, 118, 132, 126, 127, 128, 129, 138, 139, 140, 141, 147a.

Title-page: detail of the sculptures of the temple of Quetzalcoatl at Teotihuacan.

Printed by Istituto Italiano d'Arti Grafiche, Bergamo

An aspect of the Mexican coast on the Atlantic (entrance of the bay of Acapulco).

1 - Ancient Mexico. - Climate and Products. - Primitive races. - Aztec Empire.

Of all that extensive empire which once acknowledged the authority of Spain in the New World, no portion, for interest and importance, can be compared with Mexico;— and this equally, whether we consider the variety of its soil and climate; the inexhaustible stores of its mineral wealth; its scenery, grand and picturesque beyond example; the character of its ancient inhabitants, not only far surpassing in intelligence that of the other North American races, but reminding us, by their monuments, of the primitive civilization of Egypt and Hindostan; or lastly, the peculiar circumstances of its Conquest, adventurous and romantic as any legend devised by Norman or Italian bard of chivalry. It is the purpose of the present narrative to exhibit the history of this Conquest, and that of the remarkable man by whom it was achieved.

But, in order that the reader may have a better understanding of the subject, it will be well, before entering on it, to take a general survey of the political and social institutions of the races who occupied the land at the time of its discovery.

The country of the ancient Mexicans, or Aztecs as they were called, formed but a very small part of the extensive territories comprehended in the modern republic of Mexico. Its boundaries cannot be defined with certainty. They were much enlarged in the latter days of the empire, when they may be considered as reaching from about the eighteenth degree north, to the twenty-first, on the Atlantic; and from the fourteenth to the nineteenth, including

5

a very narrow strip, on the Pacific. In its greatest breadth, it could not exceed five degrees and a half, dwindling, as it approached its south-eastern limits, to less than two. It covered, probably, less than sixteen thousand square leagues. Yet such is the remarkable formation of this country, that, though not more than twice as large as New England, it presented every variety of climate, and was capable of yielding nearly every fruit, found between the equator and the Arctic circle.

All along the Atlantic, the country is bordered by a broad tract, called the *tierra caliente,* or hot region, which has the usual high temperature of equinoctial lands. Parched and sandy plains are intermingled with others, of exuberant fertility, almost impervious from thickets of aromatic shrubs and wild flowers, in the midst of which tower up trees of that magnificent growth which is found only within the tropics. In this wilderness of sweets lurks the fatal *malaria,* engendered, probably, by the decomposition of rank vegetable substances in a hot and humid soil. The season of the bilious fever,—*vómito,* as it is called,—which scourges these coasts, continues from the spring to the autumnal equinox, when it is checked by the cold winds that descend from Hudson's Bay. These winds in the winter season frequently freshen into tempests, and, sweeping down the Atlantic coast, and the winding Gulf of Mexico, burst with the fury of a hurricane on its unprotected shores, and on the neighboring West India islands. Such are the mighty spells with which Nature has surrounded this land of enchantment, as if to guard the golden treasures locked up within its bosom. The genius and enterprise of man have proved more potent than her spells.

After passing some twenty leagues across this burning region, the traveller finds himself rising into a purer atmosphere. His limbs recover their elasticity. He breathes more freely, for his senses are not now oppressed by the sultry heats and intoxicating perfumes of the valley. The aspect of nature, too, has changed, and his eye no longer revels among the gay variety of colors with which the landscape was painted there. The vanilla, the indigo, and the flowering cacao-groves disappear as he advances. The sugar-cane and the glossy-leaved banana still accompany him; and, when he has ascended about four thousand feet, he sees in the unchanging verdure, and the rich foliage of the liquid-amber tree, that he has reached the height where clouds and mists settle, in their passage from the Mexican Gulf. This is the region of perpetual humidity; but he welcomes it with pleasure, as announcing his escape from the influence of the deadly *vómito.* He has entered the *tierra templada,* or temperate region, whose character resembles that of the temperate zone of the globe. The features of the scenery become grand, and even terrible. His road sweeps along the base of mighty mountains, once gleaming with volcanic fires, and still resplendent in their mantles of snow, which serve as beacons to the mariner, for many a league at sea. All around he beholds traces of their ancient combustion, as his road passes along vast tracts of lava, bristling in the innumerable fantastic forms into which the fiery torrent has been thrown by the obstacles in its career. Perhaps, at the same moment, as he casts his eye down some steep slope, or almost unfathomable ravine, on the margin of the road, he sees their depths glowing with the rich blooms and enamelled vegetation of the tropics. Such are the singular contrasts presented at the same time, to the senses, in this picturesque region!

Still pressing upwards, the traveller mounts into other climates, favorable to other kinds of cultivation. The yellow maize, or Indian corn, as we usually call it, has continued to follow him up from the lowest level; but he now first sees fields of wheat, and the other

A characteristic landscape of Mexico and remains of an ancient colonnade.

European grains brought into the country by the Conquerors. Mingled with them, he views the plantations of the aloe or maguey *(agave Americana),* applied to such various and important uses by the Aztecs. The oaks now acquire a sturdier growth, and the dark forests of pine announce that he has entered the *tierra fria,* or cold region,—the third and last of the great natural terraces into which the country is divided. When he has climbed to the height of between seven and eight thousand feet, the weary traveller sets his foot on the summit of the Cordillera of the Andes,—the colossal range, that, after traversing South America and the Isthmus of Darien, spreads out, as it enters Mexico, into that vast sheet of table-land, which maintains an elevation of more than six thousand feet, for the distance of nearly two hundred leagues, until it gradually declines in the higher latitudes of the north.

Across this mountain rampart a chain of volcanic hills stretches, in a westerly direction, of still more stupendous dimensions, forming, indeed, some of the highest land on the globe. Their peaks, entering the limits of perpetual snow, diffuse a grateful coolness over the elevated *plateaus* below; for these last, though termed 'cold', enjoy a climate, the mean temperature of which is not lower than that of the central parts of Italy. The air is exceedingly dry; the soil, though naturally good, is rarely clothed with the luxuriant vegetation of the lower regions. It frequently, indeed, has a parched and barren aspect, owing partly to the

greater evaporation which takes places on these lofty plains, through the diminished pressure of the atmosphere; and partly, no doubt, to the want of trees to shelter the soil from the fierce influence of the summer sun. In the time of the Aztecs, the table-land was thickly covered with larch, oak, cypress, and other forest trees, the extraordinary dimensions of some of which, remaining to the present day, show that the curse of barrenness in later times is chargeable more on man than on nature. Indeed, the early Spaniards made as indiscriminate war on the forest as did our Puritan ancestors, though with much less reason. After once conquering the country, they had no lurking ambush to fear from the submissive, semicivilized Indian, and were not, like our forefathers, obliged to keep watch and war for a century. This spoliation of the ground, however, is said to have been pleasing to their imaginations, as it reminded them of the plains of their own Castile,—the table-land of Europe; where the nakedness of the landscape forms the burden of every traveller's lament, who visits that country.

Midway across the continent, somewhat nearer the Pacific than the Atlantic ocean, at an elevation of nearly seven thousand five hundred feet, is the celebrated Valley of Mexico. It is of an oval form, about sixty-seven leagues in circumference, and is encompassed by a towering rampart of porphyritic rock, which nature seems to have provided, though ineffectually, to protect it from invasion.

Approaching the Pacific coast: an exuberant vegetation...

Right: The Popocatepetl and the plain of Cholula.

8

The soil, once carpeted with a beautiful verdure, and thickly sprinkled with stately trees, is often bare, and, in many places, white with the incrustation of salts, caused by the draining of the waters. Five lakes are spread over the Valley, occupying one tenth of its surface. On the opposite borders of the largest of these basins, much shrunk in its dimensions since the days of the Aztecs, stood the cities of Mexico and Texcuco, the capitals of the two most potent and flourishing states of Anahuac, whose history, with that of the mysterious races that preceded them in the country, exhibits some of the nearest approaches to civilization to be met with anciently on the North American continent.

Of these races the most conspicuous were the Toltecs. Advancing from a northerly direction, but from what region is uncertain, they entered the territory of Anahuac, probably before the close of the seventh century. Of course, little can be gleaned, with certainty, respecting a people, whose written records have perished, and who are known to us only through the traditionary legends of the nations that succeeded them. By the general agreement of these, however, the Toltecs were well instructed in agriculture, and many of the most useful mechanic arts; were nice workers of metals; invented the complex arrangement of time adopted by the Aztecs; and, in short, were the true fountains of the civilization which distinguished this part of the continent in later times. They established their capital at Tula, north of the Mexican Valley, and the remains of extensive buildings were to be discerned there at the time of the Conquest. The noble ruins of religious and other edifices, still to be seen in various parts of New Spain, are referred to this people, whose name, *Toltec,* has passed into a synonyme for *architect.* Their shadowy history reminds us of those primitive races, who preceded the ancient Egyptians in the march of civilization; frag-

The famous "giants" of Tula: they once held up the roof of a Toltec temple.

ments of whose monuments, as they are seen at this day, incorporated with the buildings of the Egyptians themselves, give to these latter the appearance of modern constructions.

After a period of four centuries, the Toltecs, who had extended their sway over the remotest borders of Anahuac, having been greatly reduced, it is said, by famine, pestilence, and unsuccessful wars, disappeared from the land as silently and mysteriously as they had entered it. A few of them still lingered behind, but much the greater number, probably, spread over the region of Central America and the neighboring isles; and the traveller now speculates on the majestic ruins of Mitla and Palenque, as possibly the work of this extraordinary people.

After the lapse of another hundred years, a numerous and rude tribe, called the Chichemecs, entered the deserted country from the regions of the far Northwest. They were speedily followed by other races, of higher civilization, perhaps of the same family with the Toltecs, whose language they appear to have spoken. The most noted of these were the Aztecs or Mexicans, and the Acolhuans. The latter, better known in later times by the name of Tezcucans, from their capital, Tezcuco, on the eastern border of the Mexican lake, were peculiarly fitted, by their comparatively mild religion and manners, for receiving the tincture of civilization which could be derived from the few Toltecs that still remained in the country. This, in their turn, they com-

11

"The name Toltec has passed into a synonyme for architect". Above: the Toltec pyramid of Xochicalco.

municated to the barbarous Chichemecs, a large portion of whom became amalgamated with the new settlers as one nation.

Availing themselves of the strength derived, not only from this increase of numbers, but from their own superior refinement, the Acolhuans gradually stretched their empire over the ruder tribes in the north; while their capital was filled with a numerous population, busily employed in many of the more useful and even elegant arts of a civilized community. In this palmy state, they were suddenly assaulted by a warlike neighbor, the Tepanecs, their own Kindred, and inhabitants of the same valley as themselves. Their provinces were overrun, their armies beaten, their king assassinated, and the flourishing city of Tezcuco became the prize of the victor. From this abject condition the uncommon abilities of the young prince, Nezahualcoyotl, the rightful heir to the crown, backed by the efficient aid of his Mexican allies, at length, redeemed the state, and opened to it a new career of profsperity, even more brilliant than the former.

The Mexicans, with whom our history is principally concerned, came, also, as we have seen, from the remote regions of the North,— the populous hive of nations in the New World, as it has been in the Old. They arrived on the borders of Anahuac, towards the beginning of the thirteenth century, some time after the occupation of the land by the kindred races. For a long time they did not establish them-

and his broad wings opened to the rising sun. They hailed the auspicious omen, announced by the oracle, as indicating the site of their future city, and laid its foundations by sinking piles into the shallows; for the low marshes were half buried under water. On these they erected their light fabrics of reeds and rushes; and sought a precarious subsistence from fishing, and from the wild fowl which frequented the waters, as well as from the cultivation of such simple vegetables as they could raise on their floating gardens. The place was called Tenochtitlan, in token of its miraculous origin, though only known to Europeans by its other name of Mexico, derived from their war-god, Mexitli. The legend of its foundation is still further commemorated by the device of the eagle and the cactus, which form the arms of the modern Mexican republic. Such were the humble beginnings of the Venice of the Western World.

The forlorn condition of the new settlers was made still worse by domestic feuds. A

"The Mexicans arrived on the borders of Ana-huac towards the beginning of the thirteenth century".—Their migration, from a Codex.

selves in any permanent residence; but continued shifting their quarters to different parts of the Mexican Valley, enduring all the casualties and hardships of a migratory life. On one occasion, they were enslaved by a more powerful tribe; but their ferocity soon made them formidable to their masters. After a series of wanderings and adventures, which need not shrink from comparison with the most extravagant legends of the heroic ages of antiquity, they at length halted on the southwestern borders of the principal lake, in the year 1325. They there beheld, perched on the stem of a prickly pear, which shot out from the crevice of a rock that was washed by the waves, a royal eagle of extraordinary size and beauty, with a serpent in his talons,

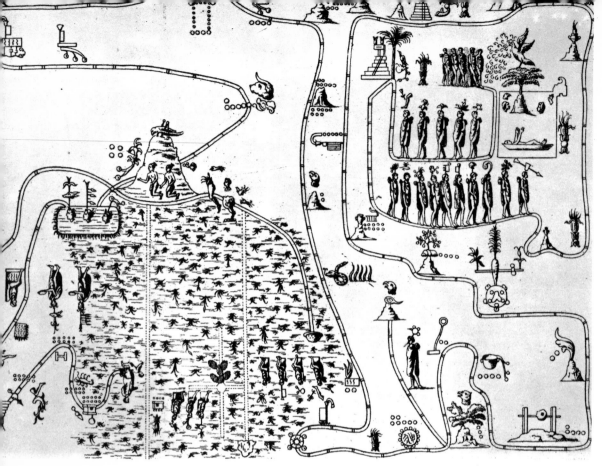

"... A series of wanderings and adventures which need not shrink from comparison with the most extravagant legends of the heroic ages of antiquity": the arrival of the Aztecs in the region of Mexico, from one of their manuscripts.

part of the citizens seceded from the main body, and formed a separate community on the neighboring marshes. Thus divided, it was long before they could aspire to the acquisition of territory on the main land. They gradually increased, however, in numbers, and strengthened themselves yet more by various improvements in their polity and military discipline, while they established a reputation for courage as well as cruelty in war, which made their name terrible throughout the Valley. In the early part of the fifteenth century, nearly a hundred years from the foundation of the city, an event took place which created an entire revolution in the circumstances, and, to some

extent, in the character of the Aztecs. This was the subversion of the Tezcucan monarchy by the Tepanecs, already noticed. When the oppressive conduct of the victors had at length aroused a spirit of resistance, its prince, Nezahualcoyotl, succeeded, after incredible perils and escapes, in mustering such a force, as, with the aid of the Mexicans, placed him on a level with his enemies. In two successive battles, these were defeated with great slaughter, their chief slain, and their territory, by one of those sudden reverses which characterize the wars of petty states, passed into the hands of the conquerors. It was awarded to Mexico, in return for its important services.

14

Then was formed that remarkable league, which, indeed, has no parallel in history. It was agreed between the states of Mexico, Tezcuco, and the neighboring little kingdom of Tlacopan, that they should mutually support each other in their wars, offensive and defensive, and that, in the distribution of the spoil, one fifth should be assigned to Tlacopan, and the remainder be divided, in what proportions is uncertain, between the other powers. The Tezcucan writers claim an equal share for their nation with the Aztecs. But this does not seem to be warranted by the immense increase of territory subsequently appropriated by the latter. And we may account for any advantage conceded to them by the treaty, on the supposition, that, however inferior they may have been originally, they were, at the time of making it, in a more prosperous condition than their allies, broken and dispirited by long oppression. What is more extraordinary than the treaty itself, however, is the fidelity with which it was maintained. During a century of uninterrupted warfare that ensued, no instance occurred where the parties quarrelled over the division of the spoil, which so often makes shipwreck of similar confederacies among civilized states.

The allies for some time found sufficient occupation for their arms in their own valley; but they soon overleaped its rocky ramparts, and by the middle of the fifteenth century under the first Montezuma had spread down the sides of the table-land to the borders of the Gulf of Mexico. Tenochtitlan, the Aztec capital, gave evidence of the public prosperity. Its frail tenements were supplanted by solid structures of stone and lime. Its population rapidly increased. Its old feuds were healed. The citizens who had seceded were again

"(The immigrants) laid the foundations (of their new city) by sinking piles into the shallows".—The site of Mexico.

15

brought under a common government with the main body and the quarter they occupied was permanently connected with the parent city; the dimensions of which, covering the same ground, were much larger than those of the modern capital of Mexico.

Fortunately, the throne was filled by a succession of able princes, who knew how to profit by their enlarged resources and by the martial enthusiasm of the nation. Year after year saw them return, loaded with the spoils of conquered cities, and with throngs of devoted captives, to their capital. No state was able long to resist the accumulated strength of the confederates. At the beginning of the sixteenth century, just before the arrival of the Spaniards, the Aztec dominion reached across the continent, from the Atlantic to the Pacific; and, under the bold and bloody Ahuitzotl, its arms had been carried far over the limits already noticed as defining its permanent territory, into the farthest corners of Guatemala and Nicaragua. This extent of empire, however limited in comparison with that of many other states, is truly wonderful, considering it as the acquisition of a people whose whole population and resources had so recently been comprised within the walls of their own petty city; and considering, moreover, that the conquered territory was thickly settled by various races, bred to arms like the Mexicans, and little inferior to them in

social organization. The history of the Aztecs suggests some strong points of resemblance to that of the ancient Romans, not only in their military successes, but in their policy.

At Teotihuacan: the Sacred Way, the square of the Moon and the Pyramid of the Sun. This view was taken from the top of the Pyramid of the Sun.

Below: Aztec statuette. "The history of the Aztecs suggests some strong points of resemblance to that of the ancient Romans".

2 - Succession to the Crown. - Aztec Nobility. - Judicial System. - Laws and Revenues. - Military Institutions.

The form of government differed in the different states of Anahuac. With the Aztecs and Tezcucans it was monarchical and nearly absolute. The two nations resembled each other so much, in their political institutions, that one of their historians has remarked, in too unqualified a manner indeed, that what is told of one may be always understood as applying to the other. I shall direct my inquiries to the Mexican polity, borrowing an illustration occasionally from that of the rival kingdom.

The government was an elective monarchy. Four of the principal nobles, who had been chosen by their own body in the preceding reign, filled the office of electors, to whom were added, with merely an honorary rank however, the two royal allies of Tezcuco and Tlacopan. The sovereign was selected from the brothers of the deceased prince, or, in default of them, from his nephews. Thus the election was always restricted to the same family. The candidate preferred must have distinguished himself in war, though, as in the case of the last Montezuma he were a member of the priesthood. This singular mode of supplying the throne had some advantages. The candidates received an education which fitted them for the royal dignity, while the age, at which they were chosen, not only secured the nation against the evils of minority, but afforded ample means for estimating their qualifications for the office. The result, at all events, was favorable; since the throne, as already noticed, was filled by a succession of able princes, well qualified to rule over a warlike and ambitious people. The scheme of election, however defective, argues a more refined and calculating policy than was to have been expected from a barbarous nation.

The new monarch was installed in his regal dignity with much parade of religious ceremony; but not until, by a victorious campaign he had obtained a sufficient number of captives to grace his triumphal entry into the capital, and to furnish victims for the dark and bloody rites which stained the Aztec superstition. Amidst this pomp of human sacrifice, he was crowned. The crown, resembling a mitre in its form, and curiously ornamented with gold, gems, and feathers, was placed on his head by the lord of Tezcuco, the most powerful of his royal allies. The title of *King,* by which the earlier Aztec princes are distinguished by Spanish writers, is supplanted by that of *Emperor* in the later reigns, intimating, perhaps, his superiority over the confederated monarchies of Tlacopan and Tezcuco.

The Aztec princes, especially towards the close of the dynasty, lived in a barbaric pomp, truly Oriental. Their spacious palaces were provided with halls for the different councils, who aided the monarch in the transaction of business. The chief of these was a sort of privy council, composed in part, probably, of the four electors chosen by the nobles after the accession, whose places, when made vacant by death, were immediately supplied as before. It was the business of this body, so far as can be gathered from the very loose accounts given of it, to advise the king, in respect to the government of the provinces, the administration of the revenues, and, indeed, on all great matters of public interest.

In the royal buildings were accommodations, also, for a numerous body-guard of the sovereign, made up of the chief nobility. It is not easy to determine with precision, in these barbarian governments, the limits of the several orders. It is certain, there was a distinct class of nobles, with large landed possessions, who held the most important

Figure of a pre-Aztec period (Museum of Anthropology of Mexico).

19

"The new monarch was installed in his regal dignity with much parade of religious ceremony... the crown resembled a mitre in its form"—The coronation of Montezuma (from an old manuscrit, National Library of Madrid).

offices near the person of the prince, and engrossed the administration of the provinces and cities. Many of these could trace their descent from the founders of the Aztec monarchy. According to some writers of authority, there were thirty great *caciques,* who had their residence, at least a part of the year, in the capital, and who could muster a hundred thousand vassals each on their estates. Without relying on such wild statements, it is clear, from the testimony of the Conquerors, that the country was occupied by numerous powerful chieftains, who lived like independent princes on their domains. If it be true that the kings encouraged, or, indeed, exacted, the residence of these nobles in the capital, and required hostages in their

absence, it is evident that their power must have been very formidable.

Their estates appear to have been held by various tenures, and to have been subject to different restrictions. Some of them, earned by their own good swords or received as the recompense of public services, were held without any limitation, except that the possessors could not dispose of them to a plebeian. Others were entailed on the eldest male issue and, in default of such, reverted to the crown. Most of them seem to have been burdened with the obligation of military service. The principal chiefs of Tezcuco, according to its chronicler, were expressly obliged to support their prince with their armed vassals, to attend his court, and aid him in the council. Some, instead of these services, were to provide for the repairs of his buildings, and to keep the royal demesnes in order, with an annual offering, by way of homage, of fruits and flowers. It was usual, if we are to believe historians, for a new king, on his accession, to confirm the investiture of estates derived from the crown.

It cannot be denied that we recognise, in all this, several features of the feudal system, which, no doubt, lose nothing of their effect, under the hands of the Spanish writers, who are fond of tracing analogies to European institutions. But such analogies lead sometimes to very erroneous conclusions. The obligation of military service, for instance, the most essential principle of a fief, seems to be naturally demanded by every government from its subjects. As to minor points of resemblance, they fall far short of that harmonious system of reciprocal service and protection, which embraced, in nice gradation, every order of a feudal monarchy. The kingdoms of Anahuac were, in their nature, despotic, attended, indeed, with many mitigating circumstances unknown to the despotisms of the East; but it is chimerical to look for much in common—beyond a few accidental forms and ceremonies—with those aristocratic institutions of the Middle Ages, which made the court of every petty baron the precise image in miniature of that of his sovereign.

The legislative power, both in Mexico and Tezcuco, resided wholly with the monarch. This feature of despotism, however, was, in some measure, counteracted by the constitution of the judicial tribunals,—of more importance, among a rude people, than the legislative, since it is easier to make good laws for such a community, than to enforce them, and the best laws, badly administered, are but a mockery. Over each of the principal cities, with its dependent territories, was placed a

The emperor Montezuma: he was king at the time of the Spanish invasion.

supreme judge, appointed by the crown, with original and final jurisdiction in both civil and criminal cases. There was no appeal from his sentence to any other tribunal, nor even to the king. He held his office during life; and any one, who usurped his ensigns, was punished with death.

Below this magistrate was a court, established in each province, and consisting of three members. It held concurrent jurisdiction with the supreme judge in civil suits, but, in criminal, an appeal lay to his tribunal. Besides these courts, there was a body of inferior magistrates, distributed through the country, chosen by the people themselves in their several districts. Their authority was limited to smaller causes, while the more important were carried up· to the higher courts. There was still another class of subordinate officers, appointed also by the people, each of whom was to watch over the conduct of a certain number of families, and report any disorder or breach of the laws to the higher authorities.

In Tezcuco the judicial arrangements were of a more refined character; and a gradation of tribunals finally terminated in a general meeting or parliament, consisting of all the judges, great and petty, throughout the kingdom, held every eighty days in the capital, over which the king presided in person. This body determined all suits, which, from their importance, or difficulty, had been reserved for its consideration by the lower tribunals. It served, moreover, as a council of state, to assist the monarch in the transaction of public business.

"The Aztec princes lived in a barbaric pomp, truly Oriental."—A nobleman, from a Codex. Right: Montezuma on his throne.

Such are the vague and imperfect notices that can be gleaned, respecting the Aztec tribunals, from the hieroglyphical paintings still preserved, and from the most accredited Spanish writers. These, being usually ecclesiastics, have taken much less interest in this subject, than in matters connected with religion. They find some apology, certainly, in the early destruction of most of the Indian paintings, from which their information was, in part, to be gathered.

On the whole, however, it must be inferred, that the Aztecs were sufficiently civilized to evince a solicitude for the rights both of property and of persons. The law, authorizing an appeal to the highest judicature in criminal matters only, shows an attention to personal security, rendered the more obligatory by the extreme severity of their penal code, which would naturally have made them more cautious of a wrong conviction. The existence of a number of coördinate tribunals, without a central one of supreme authority to control the whole, must have given rise to very discordant interpretations of the law in different districts. But this is an evil which they shared in common with most of the nations of Europe.

The provision for making the superior judges wholly independent of the crown was worthy of an enlightened people. It presented the strongest barrier, that a mere constitution could afford, against tyranny. It is not, indeed, to be supposed, that, in a government otherwise so despotic, means could not be found for influencing the magistrate. But it was a great step to fence round his authority with the sanctions of the law; and no one of the Aztec monarchs, as far as I know, is accused of an attempt to violate it.

To receive presents or a bribe, to be guilty of collusion in any way with a suitor, was punished, in a judge, with death. Who, or what tribunal, decided as to his guilt, does not appear. In Tezcuco this was done by the rest

of the court. But the king presided over that body. The Tezcucan prince, Nezahualpilli, who rarely tempered justice with mercy, put one judge to death for taking a bribe, and another for determining suits in his own house, —a capital offence, also, by law.

The judges of the higher tribunals were maintained from the produce of a part of the crown lands, reserved for this purpose. They, as well as the supreme judge, held their offices for life. The proceedings in the courts were conducted with decency and order. The judges wore an appropriate dress, and attended to business both parts of the day, dining, always, for the sake of despatch, in an apartment of the same building where they held their session; a method of proceedings much commended by the Spanish chroniclers, to whom despatch was not very familiar in their own tribunals. Officers attended to preserve order, and others summoned the parties, and produced them in court. No counsel was employed; the parties stated their own case, and supported it by their witnesses. The oath of the accused was also admitted in evidence. The statement of the case, the testimony, and the proceedings of the trial, were all set forth by a clerk, in hieroglyphical paintings, and handed over to the court. The paintings were executed with so much accuracy, that, in all suits respecting real property, they were allowed to be produced as good authority in the Spanish tribunals, very long after the Conquest; and a chair for their study and interpretation was established at Mexico in 1553, which has long since shared the fate of most other provisions for learning in that unfortunate country.

Statuette, in the courtyard of the Museum of Mexico.
Next pages: Sitting figure, coming from the western parts of ancient Mexico.—Remains of a noble mansion.

A capital sentence was indicated by a line traced with an arrow across the portrait of the accused. In Tezcuco, where the king presided in the court, this, according to the national chronicler, was done with extraordinary parade. His description, which is of rather a poetical cast, I give in his own words. "In the royal palace of Tezcuco was a court-yard, on the opposite sides of which were two halls of justice. In the principal one, called the "tribunal of God", was a throne of pure gold, inlaid with turquoises and other precious stones. On a stool, in front, was placed a human skull, crowned with an immense emerald, of a pyramidal form, and surmounted by an aigrette of brilliant plumes and precious stones. The skull was laid on a heap of military weapons, shields, quivers, bows, and arrows. The walls were hung with tapestry, made of the hair of different wild animals, of rich and various colors, festooned by gold rings, and embroidered with figures of birds and flowers. Above the throne was a canopy of variegated plumage, from the centre of which shot forth resplendent rays of gold and jewels. The other tribunal called "the King's", was also surmounted by a gorgeous canopy of feathers, on which were emblazoned the royal arms. Here the sovereign gave public audience, and communicated his despatches. But, when he decided important causes, or confirmed a capital sentence, he passed to the "tribunal of God", attended by the fourteen great lords of the realm, marshalled according to their rank. Then, putting on his mitred crown, incrusted with precious stones, and holding a golden arrow, by way of sceptre, in his left hand, he laid his right upon the skull, and pronounced judgment". All this looks rather fine for a court of justice, it must be owned. But it is certain, that the Tezcucans, as we shall see hereafter, possessed both the materials, and the skill requisite to work them up in this manner. Had they been a little

25

347

further advanced in refinement, one might well doubt their having the bad taste to do so.

The laws of the Aztecs were registered, and exhibited to the people, in their hieroglyphical paintings. Much the larger part of them, as in every nation imperfectly civilized, relates rather to the security of persons, than of property. The great crimes against society were all made capital. Even the murder of a slave was punished with death. Adulterers, as among the Jews, were stoned to death. Thieving, according to the degree of the offence, was punished by slavery or death. Yet the Mexicans could have been under no great apprehension of this crime, since the entrances to their dwellings were not secured by bolts, or fastenings of any kind. It was a capital offence to remove the boundaries of another's lands; to alter the established measures; and for a guardian not to be able to give a good account of his ward's property. These regulations evince a regard for equity in dealings, and for private rights, which argues a considerable progress in civilization. Prodigals, who squandered their patrimony, were punished in like manner; a severe sentence, since the crime brought its adequate punishment along with it. Intemperance, which was the burden, moreover, of their religious homilies, was visited with the severest penalties; as if they had foreseen in it the consuming canker of their own, as well as of the other Indian races in later times. It was punished in the young with death, and in older persons with loss of rank and confiscation of property. Yet a decent conviviality was not meant to be proscribed at their festivals, and they possessed the means of indulging it, in a mild fermented liquor, called *pulque,* which is still popular, not only with the Indian, but the European population of the country.

The rites of marriage were celebrated with as much formality as in any Christian country; and the institution was held in such reverence, that a tribunal was instituted for the sole purpose of determining questions relating to it. Divorces could not be obtained, until authorized by a sentence of this court, after a patient hearing of the parties.

But the most remarkable part of the Aztec code was that relating to slavery. There were several descriptions of slaves: prisoners taken in war, who were almost always reserved for the dreadful doom of sacrifice; criminals, public debtors, persons who, from extreme poverty, voluntarily resigned their freedom, and children who were sold by their own parents. In the last instance, usually occasioned also by poverty, it was common for the parents, with the master's consent, to substitute others of their children successively, as they grew up; thus distributing the burden, as equally as possible, among the different members of the family. The willingness of freemen to incur the penalties of this condition is explained by the mild form in which it existed. The contract of sale was executed in the presence of at least four witnesses. The services to be exacted were limited with great precision. The slave was allowed to have his own family, to hold property, and even other slaves. His children were free. No one could be born to slavery in Mexico; an honorable distinction, not known, I believe, in any civilized community where slavery has been sanctioned. Slaves were not sold by their masters, unless when these were driven to it by poverty. They were often liberated by them at their death, and sometimes, as there was no natural repugnance founded on difference

A plebeian (National Museum of Anthropology, Mexico). "The Aztec code evinces a profound respect for the great principles of morality".

of blood and race, were married to them. Yet a refractory or vicious slave might be led into the market, with a collar round his neck, which intimated his bad character, and there be publicly sold, and, on a second sale, reserved for sacrifice.

Such are some of the most striking features of the Aztec code, to which the Tezcucan bore great resemblance. With some exceptions, it is stamped with the severity, the ferocity, indeed, of a rude people, hardened by familiarity with scenes of blood, and relying on physical, instead of moral means, for the correction of evil. Still, it evinces a profound respect for the great principles of morality, and as clear a perception of these principles as is to be found in the most cultivated nations.

The royal revenues were derived from various sources. The crown lands, which appear to have been extensive, made their returns in kind. The places in the neighborhood of the capital were bound to supply workmen and materials for building the king's palaces, and keeping them in repair. They were also to furnish fuel, provisions, and whatever was necessary for his ordinary domestic expenditure, which was certainly on no stinted scale. The principal cities, which had numerous villages and a large territory dependent on them, were distributed into districts, with each a share of the lands allotted to it, for its support. The inhabitants paid a stipulated part of the produce to the crown. The vassals of the great chiefs, also, paid a portion of their earnings into the public treasury; an arrangement not at all in the spirit of the feudal institutions.

In addition to this tax on all the agricultural produce of the kingdom, there was another on its manufactures. The nature and variety of the tributes will be best shown by an enumeration of some of the principal articles. These were cotton dresses, and mantles of featherwork exquisitely made; ornamented

29

armor; vases and plates of gold; gold dust, bands and bracelets; crystal, gilt, and varnished jars and goblets; bells, arms, and utensils of copper, reams of paper; grain, fruits, copal, amber, cochineal, cacao, wild animals and birds, timber, lime, mats, etc. In this curious medley of the most homely commodities, and the elegant superfluities of luxury, it is singular that no mention should be made of silver, the great staple of the country in later times, and the use of which was known to the Aztecs.

Garrisons were established in the larger cities,—probably those at a distance, and recently conquered,—to keep down revolt, and to enforce the payment of the tribute. Tax-gatherers were also distributed throughout the kingdom, who were recognised by their official badges, and dreaded from the merciless rigor of their exactions. By a stern law, every defaulter was liable to be taken and sold as a slave. In the capital were spacious granaries and warehouses for the reception of the tributes. A receiver-general was quartered in the palace, who rendered in an exact account of the various contributions, and watched over the conduct of the inferior agents, in whom the least malversation was summarily punished. This functionary was furnished with a map of the whole empire, with a minute specification of the imposts assessed on every part of it. These imposts, moderate under the reigns of the early princes, became so burdensome under those at the close of the dynasty, being rendered still more oppressive by the manner of collection, that they bred disaffection throughout the land, and prepared the way for its conquest by the Spaniards.

This goddess with a surprising head-dress, is protecting a nobleman.
Right: a warrior. "The great aim of the Aztec institutions, to which private discipline and public honors were alike directed, was the profession of arms".

Communication was maintained with the remotest parts of the country by means of couriers. Post-houses were established on the great roads about two leagues distant from each other. The courier, bearing his despatches in the form of a hieroglyphical painting, ran with them to the first station, where they were taken by another messenger and carried forward to the next, and so on till they reached the capital. These couriers, trained from childhood, travelled with incredible swiftness; not four or five leagues an hour, as an old chronicler would make us believe, but with such speed that despatches were carried from one to two hundred miles a day. Fresh fish was frequently served at Montezuma's table in twenty-four hours from the time it had been taken in the Gulf of Mexico, two hundred miles from the capital. In this way intelligence of the movements of the royal armies was rapidly brought to court; and the dress of the courier, denoting by its color that of his tidings, spread joy or consternation in the towns through which he passed.

But the great aim of the Aztec institutions, to which private discipline and public honors were alike directed, was the profession of arms. In Mexico, as in Egypt, the soldier shared with the priest the highest consideration. The king, as we have seen, must be an experienced warrior. The tutelary deity of the Aztecs was the god of war. A great object of their military expeditions was, to gather hecatombs of captives for his altars. The soldier who fell in battle, was transported at once to the region of ineffable bliss in the bright mansions of the Sun. Every war, therefore, became a crusade; and the warrior, animated by a religious enthusiasm, like that of the early Saracen, or the Christian crusader, was not only raised to a contempt of danger, but courted it, for the imperishable crown of martyrdom. Thus we find the same impulse acting in the most opposite quarters of the globe, and the Asiatic,

31

Left: The sculpture on this column at Tula represents a warrior.
Right: another warrior.

61436

the European, and the American, each earnestly invoking the holy name of religion in the perpetration of human butchery.

The question of war was discussed in a council of the king and his chief nobles. Ambassadors were sent, previously to its declaration, to require the hostile state to receive the Mexican gods, and to pay the customary tribute. The persons of ambassadors were held sacred throughout Anahuac. They were lodged and entertained in the great towns at the public charge and were everywhere received with courtesy, so long as they did not deviate from the highroads on their route. When they did, they forfeited their privileges. If the embassy proved unsuccessful, a defiance, or open declaration of war, was sent; quotes were drawn from the conquered provinces, which were always subjected to military service, as well as the payment of taxes; and the royal army, usually with the monarch at his head, began its march.

The Aztec princes made use of the incentive employed by European monarchs to excite the ambition of their followers. They established various military orders, each having its privileges and peculiar insignia. There seems, also, to have existed a sort of knighthood, of inferior degree. It was the cheapest reward of martial prowess and whoever had not reached it was excluded from using ornaments on his arms or his person, and obliged to wear a coarse white stuff, made from the threads of the aloe, called *nequen*. Even the members of the royal family were not excepted from this law, which reminds one of the occasional practice of Christian knights, to wear plain armor, or shields without device, till they had achieved some doughty feat of chivalry. Although the military orders were thrown open to all, it is probable that they were chiefly filled with persons of rank, who, by their previous training and connections, were able to come

This animal sculptured on one of the sides of the north pyramid at Tula, seems to be a fox.

35

into the field under peculiar advantages.

The dress of the higher warriors was picturesque and often magnificent. Their bodies were covered with a close vest of quilted cotton, so thick as to be impenetrable to the light missiles of Indian warfare. This garment was so light and serviceable, that it was adopted by the Spaniards. The wealthier chiefs sometimes wore, instead of this cotton mail, a cuirass made of thin plates of gold, or silver. Over it was thrown a surcoat of the gorgeous feather-work in which they excelled. Their helmets were sometimes of wood, fashioned like the heads of wild animals, and sometimes of silver, on the top of which waved a *panache* of variegated plumes, sprinkled with precious stones and ornaments of gold. They wore also collars, bracelets, and earrings, of the same rich materials.

Their armies were divided into bodies of eight thousand men; and these, again, into companies of three or four hundred, each with its own commander. The national standard, which has been compared to the ancient Roman, displayed, in its embroidery of gold and feather-work, the armorial ensigns of the state. These were significant of its name, which, as the names of both persons and places were borrowed from some material object, was easily expressed by hieroglyphical symbols. The companies and the great chiefs had also their appropriate banners and devices, and the gaudy hues of their many-colored plumes gave a dazzling splendor to the spectacle.

Their tactics were such as belong to a nation, with whom war, though a trade, is not elevated to the rank of a science. They advanced singing, and shouting their war-cries, briskly charging the enemy, as rapidly retreating, and making use of ambuscades, sudden surprises, and the light skirmish of guerilla warfare. Yet their discipline was such as to draw forth the encomiums of the Spanish

conquerors. "A beautiful sight it was", says one of them, "to see them set out on their march, all moving forward so gayly, and in so admirable order!" In battle, they did not seek to kill their enemies, so much as to take them prisoners; and they never scalped, like other North American tribes. The valor of a warrior was estimated by the number of his prisoners; and no ransom was large enough to save the devoted captive.

Their military code bore the same stern features as their other laws. Disobedience of orders was punished with death. It was death, also, for a soldier to leave his colors, to attack the enemy before the signal was given, or to plunder another's booty or prisoners. One of the last Tezcucan princes, in the spirit of an ancient Roman, put two sons to death,—after having cured their wounds,—for violating the last-mentioned law.

I must not omit to notice here an institution,

The Aztec warriors, their equipment, their behavior in the battle...
"The Aztec princes established various military orders, each having its privileges and peculiar insignia".

the introduction of which, in the Old World, is ranked among the beneficent fruits of Christianity. Hospitals were established in the principal cities, for the cure of the sick, and the permanent refuge of the disabled soldier; and surgeons were placed over them, "who were so far better than those in Europe", says an old chronicler, "that they did not protract the cure, in order to increase the pay".

Such is the brief outline of the civil and military polity of the ancient Mexicans; less perfect than could be desired, in regard to the former, from the imperfection of the sources whence it is drawn. Whoever has had occasion to explore the early history of modern Europe has found how vague and unsatisfactory is the political information which can be gleaned from the gossip of monkish annalists. How much is the difficulty increased in the present instance, where this information, first recorded in the dubious language of hieroglyphics, was interpreted in another language, with which the Spanish chroniclers were imperfectly acquainted, while it related to institutions of which their past experience enabled them to form no adequate conception! Amidst such uncertain lights, it is in vain to expect nice accuracy of detail. All that can be done is, to attempt an outline of the more prominent features, that a correct impression, so far as it goes, may be produced on the reader.

Enough has been said, however, to show that the Aztec and Tezcucan races were advanced in civilization very far beyond the wandering tribes of North America. The degree of civilization which they had reached, as inferred by their political institutions, may be considered, perhaps, not much short of that enjoyed by our Saxon ancestors, under Alfred. In respect to the nature of it, they may be better compared with the Egyptians; and the examination of their social relations and culture may suggest still stronger points of resemblance to that ancient people.

The statuette on the left represents a warrior. Above: a shield in feather-work. The Codex opposite shows a tribe surrendering to an Aztec chief.

Those familiar with the modern Mexicans will find it difficult to conceive that the nation should ever have been capable of devising the enlightened polity which we have been considering. But they should remember that in the Mexicans of our day they see only a conquered race; as different from their ancestors as are the modern Egyptians from those who built,—I will not say, the tasteless pyramids,—but the temples and palaces, whose magnificent wrecks strew the borders of the Nile, at Luxor and Karnac. The difference is not so great as between the ancient Greek, and his degenerate descendant, lounging among the masterpieces of art which he has scarcely taste enough to admire,—speaking the language of those still more imperishable monuments of literature which he has hardly capacity to comprehend. Yet he breathes the same atmosphere, is warmed by the same sun, nourished by the same scenes, as those who fell at Marathon, and won the trophies of Olympic Pisa. The same blood flows in his veins that flowed in theirs. But ages of tyranny have passed over him; he belongs to a conquered race.

The American Indian has something peculiarly sensitive in his nature. He shrinks instinctively from the rude touch of a foreign hand. Even when this foreign influence comes in the form of civilization, he seems to sink and pine away beneath it. It has been so with the Mexicans. Under the Spanish domination, their numbers have silently melted away. Their energies are broken. They no longer tread their mountain plains with the conscious independence of their ancestors. In their faltering step, and meek and melancholy aspect, we read the sad characters of the conquered race. The cause of humanity, indeed, has gained. They live under a better system of laws, a more assured tranquillity, a purer faith. But all does not avail. Their civilization was of the hardy character which belongs to the wilderness. The fierce virtues of the Aztec were all his own. They refused to submit to European culture,—to be engrafted on a foreign stock. His outward form, his complexion, his lineaments, are substantially the same. But the moral characteristics of the nation, all that constituted its individuality as a race, are effaced for ever.

Characteristic specimens of architectural ornaments.—"The Mexican races were advanced in civilization... they may be compared with the Egyptians".

3 - Mexican Mythology. - The sacerdotal order. - The Temples. - Human sacrifices.

The civil polity of the Aztecs is so closely blended with their religion, that, without understanding the latter, it is impossible to form correct ideas of their government or their social institutions. I shall pass over, for the present, some remarkable traditions, bearing a singular resemblance to those found in the Scriptures, and endeavour to give a brief sketch of their mythology, and their careful provisions for maintaining a national worship.

Mythology may be regarded as the poetry of religion,—or rather as the poetic development of the religious principle in a primitive age. It is the effort of untutored man to explain the mysteries of existence, and the secret agencies by which the operations of nature are conducted. Although the growth of similar conditions of society, its character must vary with that of the rude tribes in which it originates; and the ferocious Goth, quaffing mead from the skulls of his slaughtered enemies, must have a very different mythology from that of the effeminate native of Hispaniola, loitering away his hours in idle pastimes, under the shadow of his bananas.

At a later and more refined period, we sometimes find these primitive legends combined into a regular system under the hands of the poet, and the rude outline moulded into forms of ideal beauty, which are the objects of adoration in a credulous age, and the delight of all succeeding ones. Such were the beautiful inventions of Hesiod and Homer, "who", says the Father of History, "created the theogony of the Greeks"; an assertion not to be taken too literally, since it is hardly possible that any man should create a religious system for his nation. They only filled up the shadowy outlines of tradition with the bright touches of their own imaginations, until they had clothed them in beauty which kindled the imaginations of others. The power of the poet, indeed, may be felt in a similar way in a much riper period of society. To say nothing of the "Divina Commedia", who is there that rises from the perusal of "Paradise Lost", without feeling his own conceptions of the angelic hierarchy quickened by those of the inspired artist, and a new and sensible form, as it were, given to images which had before floated dim and undefined before him?

The last-mentioned period is succeeded by that of philosophy; which, disclaiming alike the legends of the primitive age, and the poetical embellishments of the succeeding one, seeks to shelter itself from the charge of impiety by giving an allegorical interpretation to the popular mythology, and thus to reconcile the latter with the genuine deductions of science.

The Mexican religion had emerged from the first of the periods we have been considering, and, although little affected by poetical influences, had received a peculiar complexion from the priests, who had digested as thorough and burdensome a ceremonial, as ever existed in any nation. They had, moreover, thrown the veil of allegory over early tradition, and invested their deities with attributes, savoring much more of the grotesque conceptions of the eastern nations in the Old World, than of the lighter fictions of Greek mythology, in which the features of humanity, however exaggerated, were never wholly abandoned.

In contemplating the religious system of the Aztecs, one is struck with its apparent incongruity, as if some portion of it had emanated from a comparatively refined people, open to gentle influences, while the rest breathes a spirit of unmitigated ferocity. It

One of the temples of Monte Alban.—"In contemplating the religious system of the Aztecs, one is struck with its apparent incongruity"...

naturally suggests the idea of two distinct sources, and authorizes the belief that the Aztecs had inherited from their predecessors a milder faith, on which was afterwards engrafted their own mythology. The latter soon become dominant, and gave its dark coloring to the creeds of the conquered nations,—which the Mexicans, like the ancient Romans, seem willingly to have incorporated into their own,—until the same funereal superstition settled over the farthest borders of Anahuac.

The Aztecs recognised the existence of a supreme Creator and Lord of the universe. They addressed him, in their prayers, as "the God by whom we live", "omnipresent, that knoweth all thoughts, and giveth all gifts", "without whom man is as nothing", "invisible, incorporeal, one God, of *perfect perfection* and purity", "under whose wings we find repose and a sure defence". These sublime attributes infer no inadequate conception of the true God. But the idea of unity—of a being, with whom volition is action, who has no need of inferior ministers to execute his purposes—was too simple, or too vast, for their understandings; and they sought relief, as usual, in a plurality of deities, who presided over the elements, the changes of the seasons, and the various occupations of man. Of these, there were thirteen principal deities, and more than two hundred inferior; to each of whom some special day, or appropriate festival, was consecrated.

At the head of all stood the terrible Huit-zilopotchli, the Mexican Mars; although it is doing injustice to the heroic war-god of antiquity to identify him with this sanguinary

"Quetzalcoatl, god of the air, was one of those benefactors of their species... Under him, the earth teemed with fruits and flowers, without the pains of culture".

44

monster. This was the patron deity of the nation. His fantastic image was loaded with costly ornaments. His temples were the most stately and august of the public edifices; and his altars reeked with the blood of human hecatombs in every city of the empire. Disastrous, indeed, must have been the influence of such a superstition on the character of the people.

A far more interesting personage in their mythology was Quetzalcoatl, god of the air, a divinity who, during his residence on earth, instructed the natives in the use of metals, in agriculture, and in the arts of government. He was one of those benefactors of their species, doubtless, who have been deified by the gratitude of posterity. Under him, the earth teemed with fruits and flowers, without the pains of culture. An ear of Indian corn was as much as a single man could carry. The cotton, as it grew, took, of its own accord, the rich dyes of human art. The air was filled with intoxicating perfumes and the sweet melody of birds. In short, these were the halcyon days, which find a place in the mythic systems of so many nations in the Old World. It was the *golden age* of Anahuac.

From some cause, not explained, Quetzalcoatl incurred the wrath of one of the principal gods and was compelled to abandon the country. On his way, he stopped at the city of Cholula, where a temple was dedicated to his worship, the massy ruins of which still form one of the most interesting relics of antiquity in Mexico. When he reached the shores of the Mexican Gulf, he took leave of his followers, promising that he and his descendants would revisit them hereafter, and then, entering his wizard skiff, made of serpents' skins, embarked on the great ocean for the fabled land of Tlapallan. He was said to have been tall in stature, with a white skin, long, dark hair, and a flowing beard. The Mexicans looked confidently to the return of

Quetzalcoatl, from an Aztec calendar.

the benevolent deity; and this remarkable tradition, deeply cherished in their hearts, prepared the way, as we shall see hereafter, for the future success of the Spaniards.

We have not space for further details respecting the Mexican divinities, the attributes of many of whom were carefully defined, as they descended, in regular gradation, to the *penates* or household gods, whose little images were to be found in the humblest dwelling.

The Aztecs felt the curiosity, common to man in almost every stage of civilization, to lift the veil which covers the mysterious past, and the more awful future. They sought relief, like the nations of the Old Continent, from the oppressive idea of eternity, by breaking it up into distinct cycles, or periods of time, each of several thousand years' duration. There were four of these cycles, and at the end of each, by the agency of the elements, the human family was swept from the earth, and the sun blotted out from the heavens, to be again rekindled.

They imagined three separate states of existence in the future life. The wicked, comprehending the greater part of mankind, were to expiate their sins in a place of everlas-

45

ting darkness. Another class, with no other merit than that of having died of certain diseases, capriciously selected, were to enjoy a negative existence of indolent contentment. The highest place was reserved, as in most warlike nations, for the heroes who fell in battle, or in sacrifice. They passed, at once, into the presence of the Sun, whom they accompanied with songs and choral dances, in his bright progress through the heavens; and, after some years, their spirits went to animate the clouds and singing birds of beautiful plumage, and to revel amidst the rich blossoms and odors of the gardens of paradise. Such was the heaven of the Aztecs; more refined in its character than that of the more polished pagan, whose elysium reflected only the martial sports, or sensual gratifications, of this life. In the destiny they assigned to the wicked, we discern similar traces of refinement; since the absence of all physical torture forms a striking contrast to the schemes of suffering so ingeniously devised by the fancies of the most enlightened nations. In all this, so contrary to the natural suggestions of the ferocious Aztec, we see the evidences of a higher civilization, inherited from their predecessors in the land.

Our limits will allow only a brief allusion to one or two of their most interesting ceremonies. On the death of a person, his corpse was dressed in the peculiar habiliments of his tutelar deity. It was strewed with pieces of paper, which operated as charms against the dangers of the dark road he was to travel. A throng of slaves, if he were rich, was sacrificed at his obsequies. His body was burned, and the ashes, collected in a vase, were preserved in one of the apartments of his house. Here

"Quetzalcoatl took leave of his followers, promising that he and his descendants would revisit them hereafter, and embarked on the great ocean. He was said to have a white skin..."—From this precise spot, according to the legend (Coatzocoalcos, picture opposite) he left Mexico.

we have successively the usages of the Roman Catholic, the Mussulman, the Tartar, and the Ancient Greek and Roman; curious coincidences, which may show how cautious we should be in adopting conclusions founded on analogy.

A more extraordinary coincidence may be traced with Christian rites, in the ceremony of naming their children. The lips and bosom of the infant were sprinkled with water, and "the Lord was implored to permit the holy drops to wash away the sin that was given to it before the foundation of the world; so that the child might be born anew". We are reminded of Christian morals, in more than one of their prayers, in which they used regular forms. "Wilt thou blot us out, O Lord, for ever? Is this punishment intended, not for our reformation, but for our destruction?" Again, "Impart to us, out of thy great mercy, thy gifts, which we are not worthy to receive through our own merits". "Keep peace with all", says another petition; "bear injuries with humility; God, who sees, will avenge you". But the most striking parallel with Scripture is in the remarkable declaration, that "he, who looks too curiously on a woman, commits adultery with his eyes". These pure and elevated maxims, it is true, are mixed up with others of a puerile, and even brutal character, arguing that confusion of the moral perceptions, which is natural in the twilight of civilization. One would not expect, however, to meet, in such a state of society, with doctrines as sublime as any inculcated by the enlightened codes of ancient philosophy.

But, although the Aztec mythology gathered nothing from the beautiful inventions of the poet, nor from the refinements of philosophy, it was much indebted, as I have noticed, to the priests, who endeavoured to dazzle the imagination of the people by the most formal and pompous ceremonial. The

47

influence of the priesthood must be greatest in an imperfect state of civilization, where it engrosses all the scanty science of the time in its own body. This is particularly the case, when the science is of that spurious kind which is less occupied with the real phenomena of nature, than with the fanciful chimeras of human superstition. Such are the sciences of astrology and divination, in which the Aztec priests were well initiated; and, while they seemed to hold the keys of the future in their own hands, they impressed the ignorant people with sentiments of superstitious awe, beyond that which has probably existed in any other country,—even in ancient Egypt.

The sacerdotal order was very numerous; as may be inferred from the statement, that five thousand priests were, in some way or other, attached to the principal temple in the capital. The various ranks and functions of this multitudinous body were discriminated with great exactness. Those best instructed in music took the management of the choirs. Others arranged the festivals conformably to the calendar. Some superintended the education of youth, and others had charge of the hieroglyphical paintings and oral traditions; while the dismal rites of sacrifice were reserved for the chief dignitaries of the order. At the head of the whole establishment were two high-priests, elected from the order, as it would seem, by the king and principal nobles, without reference to birth, but solely for their qualifications, as shown by their previous conduct in a subordinate station. They were equal in dignity, and inferior only to the sovereign, who rarely acted without their advice in weighty matters of public concern.

The priests were each devoted to the service of some particular deity, and had quarters provided within the spacious precincts of their temple; at least, while engaged

"The sacerdotal order was very numerous; as may be inferred from the statement, that five thousand priests were attached to the principal temple in the capital. The various ranks and functions of this multitudinous body were discriminated with great exactness. Those best instructed in music took the management of the choirs... the dismal rites of sacrifice were reserved for the chief dignitaries of the order." Above: an Aztec priest. Opposite: reconstitution of the temples of Tenochtitlan.

in immediate attendance there,—for they were allowed to marry, and have families of their own. In this monastic residence they lived in all the stern severity of conventual discipline. Thrice during the day, and once at night, they were called to prayers. They were frequent in their ablutions and vigils, and mortified the flesh by fasting and cruel penance,—drawing blood from their bodies by flagellation, or by piercing them with the thorns of the aloe; in short, by practising all those austerities to which fanaticism (to borrow the strong language of the poet) has resorted, in every age of the world, "In hopes to merit heaven by making earth a hell".

The great cities were divided into districts, placed under the charge of a sort of parochial clergy, who regulated every act of religion within their precincts. It is remarkable that they administered the rites of confession and absolution. The secrets of the confessional were held inviolable, and penances were imposed of much the same kind as those enjoined in the Roman Catholic Church. There were two remarkable peculiarities in the Aztec ceremony. The first was, that, as the repetition of an offence, once atoned for,

was deemed inexpliable, confession was made but once in a man's life, and was usually deferred to a late period of it, when the penitent unburdened his conscience, and settled, at once, the long arrears of iniquity. Another peculiarity was, that priestly absolution was received in place of the legal punishment of offences, and authorized an acquittal in case of arrest. Long after the Conquest, the simple natives, when they came under the arm of the law, sought to escape by producing the certificate of their confession.

One of the most important duties of the priesthood was that of education, to which certain buildings were appropriated within the inclosure of the principal temple. Here the youtb of both sexes, of the higher and middling orders, were placed at a very tender age. The girls were intrusted to the care of priestesses; for women were allowed to exercise sacerdotal functions, except those of sacrifice. In these institutions the boys were drilled in the routine of monastic discipline; they decorated the shrines of the gods with flowers, fed the sacred fires, and took part in the religious chants and festivals. Those in the higher school—the *Calmecac,* as it was

called—were initiated in their traditionary lore, the mysteries of hieroglyphics, the principles of government, and such branches of astronomical and natural science as were within the compass of the priesthood. The girls learned various feminine employments, especially to weave and embroider rich coverings for the altars of the gods. Great attention was paid to the moral discipline of both sexes. The most perfect decorum prevailed; and offences were punished with extreme rigor, in some instances with death itself. Terror, not love, was the spring of education with the Aztecs.

At a suitable age for marrying, or for entering into the world, the pupils were dismissed, with much ceremony, from the convent, and the recommendation of the principal often introduced those most competent to responsible situations in public life. Such was the crafty policy of the Mexican priests, who, by reserving to themselves the business of instruction, were enabled to mould the young and plastic mind according to their own wills, and to train it early to implicit reverence for religion and its ministers; a reverence which still maintained its hold on the iron nature of the warrior, long after every other vestige of education had been effaced by the rough trade to which he was devoted.

To each of the principal temples, lands were annexed for the maintenance of the priests. These estates were augmented by the policy or devotion of successive princes, until, under the last Montezuma, they had swollen to an enormous extent, and covered every district of the empire. The priests took the management of their property into their own hands; and they seem to have treated their tenants with the liberality and indulgence characteristic of monastic corporations. Besides the large supplies drawn from this source, the religious order was

"The Mexican temples were very numerous... They were distributed into stories. The ascent was by a flight of steps on the outside."
—"An extraordinary coincidence may be traced with Christian rites, in the ceremony of naming their children... It is remarkable that they administered the rites of confession and absolution... The secrets of the confessional were held inviolable".

enriched with the first-fruits, and such other offerings as piety or superstition dictated. The surplus beyond what was required for the support of the national worship was distributed in alms among the poor; a duty strenuously prescribed by their moral code. Thus we find the same religion inculcating lessons of pure philanthropy, on the one hand, and of merciless extermination, as we shall soon see, on the other. The inconsistency will not appear incredible to those who are familiar with the history of the Roman Catholic Church, in the early ages of the Inquisition.

The Mexican temples—*teocallis,* "houses of God", as they were called—were very numerous. There were several hundreds in each of the principal cities, many of them, doubtless, very humble edifices. They were solid masses of earth, cased with brick, or stone, and in their form somewhat resembled the pyramidal structures of ancient Egypt. The bases of many of them were more than a hundred feet square, and they towered to a still greater height. They were distributed into four of five stories, each of smaller dimensions than that below. The ascent was by a flight of steps, at an angle of the pyramid, on the outside. This led to a sort of terrace, or gallery, at the base of the second story, which passed quite round the building to another flight of stairs, commencing also at the same angle as the preceding and directly over it, and leading to a similar terrace; so that one had to make the circuit of the temple several times, before reaching the summit. In some instances the stairway led directly up the centre of the western face of the building. The top was a broad area, on which were erected one or two towers, forty or fifty feet high, the sanctuaries in which stood the sacred images of the presiding deities. Before these towers stood the dreadful stone of sacrifice, and two lofty altars, on which

A few steps of the temple of Quetzalcoatl at Teotihuacan.—"From the construction of the temples, all religious services were public. The long processions of priests, winding round their massive sides, were all visible from the remotest corners of the capital".

53

fires were kept, as inextinguishable as those in the temple of Vesta. There were said to be six hundred of these altars, on smaller buildings within the inclosure of the great temple of Mexico, which, with those on the sacred edifices in other parts of the city, shed a brilliant illumination over its streets, through the darkest night.

From the construction of their temples, all religious services were public. The long processions of priests, winding round their massive sides, as they rose higher and higher towards the summit, and the dismal rites of sacrifice performed there, were all visible from the remotest corners of the capital, impressing on the spectator's mind a superstitious veneration for the mysteries of his

... decorating the great sanctuary of Teotihuacan.

Heads of plumed serpents...

religion, and for the dread ministers by whom they were interpreted.

This impression was kept in full force by their numerous festivals. Every month was consecrated to some protecting deity; and every week, nay, almost every day, was set down in their calendar for some appropriate celebration; so that it is difficult to understand how the ordinary business of life could have been compatible with the exactions of religion. Many of their ceremonies were of a light and cheerful complexion, consisting of the national songs and dances, in which both sexes joined. Processions were made of women and children crowned with garlands and bearing offerings of fruits, the ripened maize, or the sweet incense of copal and other odoriferous gums, while the altars of the deity were stained with no blood save that of animals. These were the peaceful rites derived from their Toltec predecessors, on which the fierce Aztecs engrafted a superstition too loathsome to be exhibited in all its

54

nakedness, and one over which I would gladly draw a veil altogether, but that it would leave the reader in ignorance of their most striking institution, and one that had the greatest influence in forming the national character.

Human sacrifices were adopted by the Aztecs early in the fourteenth century, about two hundred years before the Conquest. Rare at first, they became more frequent with the wider extent of their empire; till, at length, almost every festival was closed with this cruel abomination. These religious ceremonials were generally arranged in such a manner as to afford a type of the most prominent circumstances in the character or history of the deity who was the object of them. A single example will suffice.

One of their most important festivals was that in honor of the god, Tezcatlipoca, whose rank was inferior only to that of the Supreme Being. He was called "the soul of the world", and supposed to have been its creator. He was depicted as a handsome man, endowed with perpetual youth. A year before the intended sacrifice, a captive, distinguished for his personal beauty, and without a blemish on his body, was selected to represent this deity. Certain tutors took charge of him, and instructed him how to perform his new part with becoming grace and dignity. He was arrayed in a splendid dress, regaled with incense and with a profusion of sweet-scented flowers, of which the ancient Mexicans were

"Many of their ceremonies were of a light and cheerful complexion consisting of the national songs and dances, in which both sexes joined". These statuettes of pre-Aztec art evoke a gathering of men making an offering.

"Human sacrifices have been practised by many nations... but never by any, on a scale to be compared with those in Anahuac. (The authors give an estimation) of twenty thousand victims a year, and some carry the number as high as fifty!".

as fond as their descendants at the present day. When he went abroad, he was attended by a train of the royal pages, and, as he halted in the streets to play some favorite melody, the crowd prostrated themselves before him, and did him homage as the representative of their good deity. In this way he led an easy, luxurious life, till within a month of his sacrifice. Four beautiful girls, bearing the names of the principal goddesses, were then selected to share the honors of his bed; and with them he continued to live in idle dalliance, feasted at the banquets of the principal nobles, who paid him all the honors of a divinity.

At length the fatal day of sacrifice arrived. The term of his short-lived glories was at an end. He was stripped of his gaudy apparel, and bade adieu to the fair partners of his revelries. One of the royal barges transported him across the lake to a temple which rose on its margin, about a league from the city. Hither the inhabitants of the capital flocked, to witness the consummation of the ceremony. As the sad procession wound up the sides of the pyramid, the unhappy victim threw away his gay chaplets of flowers, and broke in pieces the musical instruments with which he had solaced the hours of captivity. On the summit he was received by six priests, whose long and matted locks flowed disorderly over their sable robes, covered with hieroglyphic scrolls of mystic import. They led

The sacrificial stone in the great pyramid of Mexico.—"(A priest), clad in a scarlet mantle, opened the breast of the wretched victim with a sharp razor of itztli, a volcanic substance... and tore out the palpitating heart, holding this up towards the sun".

him to the sacrificial stone, a huge block of jasper, with its upper surface somewhat convex. On this the prisoner was stretched. Five priests secured his head and his limbs; while the sixth, clad in a scarlet mantle, emblematic of his bloody office, dexterously opened the breast of the wretched victim with a sharp razor of *itztli,*—a volcanic substance, hard as flint,—and, inserting his hand in the wound, tore out the palpitating heart. The minister of death, first holding this up towards the sun, an object of worship throughout Anahuac, cast it at the feet of the deity to whom the temple was devoted, while the multitudes below prostrated themselves in humble adoration. The tragic story of this prisoner was expounded by the priests as the type of human destiny, which, brilliant in its commencement, too often closes in sorrow and disaster.

Such was the form of human sacrifice usually practised by the Aztecs. It was the same that often met the indignant eyes of the Europeans, in their progress through the country, and from the dreadful doom of which they themselves were not exempted. There were, indeed, some occasions when preliminary tortures, of the most exquisite kind,—with which it is unnecessary to shock the reader,—were inflicted, but they always terminated with the bloody ceremony above described. It should be remarked, however,

57

"At the dedication of the great temple of Huitzilopotchli, seventy thousand captives are said to have perished at the shrine of this terrible deity!... The ceremony consumed several days"—This imposing sacrificial stone can be seen in the Museum of Mexico.

that such tortures were not the spontaneous suggestions of cruelty, as with the North American Indians; but were all rigorously prescribed in the Aztec ritual, and doubtless were often inflicted with the same compunctious visitings which a devout familiar of the Holy Office might at times experience in executing its stern decrees. Women, as well as the other sex, were sometimes reserved for sacrifice. On some occasions, particularly in seasons of drought, at the festival of the insatiable Tlaloc, the god of rain, children, for the most part infants, were offered up. As they were borne along in open litters, dressed in their festal robes, and decked with the fresh blossoms of spring, they moved the hardest heart to pity, though their cries were drowned in the wild chant of the priests, who read in their tears a favorable augury for their petition. These innocent victims were generally bought by the priests of parents who were poor, but who stifled the voice of nature, probably less at the suggestions of poverty, than of a wretched superstition.

The most loathsome part of the story—the manner in which the body of the sacrificed captive was disposed of—remains yet to be told. It was delivered to the warrior who had taken him in battle, and by him, after being dressed, was served up in an entertainment to his friends. This was not the coarse repast of famished cannibals, but a banquet teeming with delicious beverages and delicate viands, prepared with art, and attended by both sexes, who, as we shall see hereafter, conducted themselves with all the decorum of civilized life. Surely, never were refinement and the extreme of barbarism brought so closely in contact with each other!

Human sacrifices have been practised by many nations, not excepting the most polished nations of antiquity; but never by any, on a scale to be compared with those in Anahuac. The amount of victims immolated on its accursed altars would stagger the faith of the least scupulous believer. Scarcely any author pretends to estimate the yearly sacrifices throughout the empire at less than twenty thousand, and some carry the number as high as fifty!

On great occasions, as the coronation of a king, or the consecration of a temple, the number becomes still more appalling. At the dedication of the great temple of Huitzilopotchli, in 1486, the prisoners, who for some years had been reserved for the purpose, were drawn from all quarters to the capital.

Detail of one of the ornaments on the sacrificial stone presented on the page before.

They were ranged in files, forming a procession nearly two miles long. The ceremony consumed several days, and seventy thousand captives are said to have perished at the shrine of this terrible deity! But who can believe that so numerous a body would have suffered themselves to be led unresistingly like sheep to the slaughter? Or how could their remains, too great for consumption in the ordinary way, be disposed of, without breeding a pestilence in the capital? Yet the event was of recent date, and is unequivocally attested by the best informed historians. One fact may be considered certain. It was customary to preserve the skulls of the sacrificed, in buildings appropriated to the purpose. The companions of Cortés counted one hundred and thirty-six thousand in one of these edifices! Without attempting a precise calculation, therefore, it is safe to conclude that thousands were yearly offered up, in the different cities of Anahuac, on the bloody altars of the Mexican divinities.

Indeed, the great object of war, with the Aztecs, was quite as much to gather victims for their sacrifices, as to extend their empire. Hence it was, that an enemy was never slain in battle, if there were a chance of taking him alive. To this circumstance the Spaniards repeatedly owed their preservation. When Montezuma was asked, "why he had suffered the republic of Tlascala to maintain her independence on his borders", he replied, "that she might furnish him with victims for his gods!" As the supply began to fail, the priests, the Dominicans of the New World, bellowed aloud for more, and urged on their superstitious sovereign by the denunciations of celestial wrath. Like the militant churchmen of Christendom in the Middle Ages, they mingled themselves in the ranks, and were conspicuous in the thickest of the fight, by their hideous aspect and frantic gestures. Strange, that, in every country, the most

fiendish passions of the human heart have been those kindled in the name of religion!

The influence of these practices on the Aztec character was as disastrous as might have been expected. Familiarity with the bloody rites of sacrifice steeled the heart against human sympathy, and begat a thirst for carnage, like that excited in the Romans by the exhibitions of the circus. The perpetual recurrence of ceremonies, in which the people took part, associated religion with their most intimate concerns, and spread the gloom of superstition over the domestic hearth, until the character of the nation wore a grave and even melancholy aspect, which belongs to their descendants at the present day. The influence of the priesthood, of course, became unbounded. The sovereign thought himself honored by being permitted to assist in the services of the temple. Far from limiting the authority of the priests to spiritual matters, he often surrendered his opinion to theirs, where they were least competent to give it. It was their opposition that prevented the final capitulation which would have saved the capital. The whole nation, from the peasant to the prince, bowed their necks to the worst kind of tyranny, that of a blind fanaticism.

In reflecting on the revolting usages recorded in the preceding pages, one finds it difficult to reconcile their existence with any thing like a regular form of government, or an advance in civilization. Yet the Mexicans had many claims to the character of a civilized community. One may, perhaps, better understand the anomaly, by reflecting on the condition of some of the most polished countries in Europe, in the sixteenth century, after the establishment of the modern Inquisition; an institution, which yearly destroyed its thousands, by a death more painful than the Aztec sacrifices.

Human sacrifice, however cruel, has nothing in it degrading to its victim. It may

Left: is this elaborate head-dress, are these feather ornaments, the insignia of a nobleman? Above: skull in a wall of the great temple of Mexico.

not feed on human flesh merely to gratify a brutish appetite, but in obedience to their religion. Their repasts were made of the victims whose blood had been poured out on the altar of sacrifice. This is a distinction worthy of notice. Still, cannibalism, under any form, or whatever sanction, cannot but have a fatal influence on the nation addicted to it. It suggests ideas so loathsome, so degrading to man, to his spiritual and immortal nature, that it is impossible the people who practise it should make any great progress in moral or intellectual culture. The Mexicans furnish no exception to this remark. The civilization, which they possessed, descended from the Toltecs, a race who never stained their altars, still less their banquets, with the blood of man. All that deserved the name of science in Mexico came from this source; and the crumbling ruins of edifices, attributed to them, still extant in various parts of New Spain, show a decided superiority in their architecture over that of the later races of Anahuac. It is true, the Mexicans made great proficiency in many of the social and mechanic arts. In purely intellectual progress, they were behind the Tezcucans, whose wise sovereigns came into the abominable rites of their neighbors with reluctance, and practised them on a much more moderate scale.

In this state of things, it was beneficently ordered by Providence that the land should be delivered over to another race, who would rescue it from the brutish superstitions that daily extended wider and wider, with extent of empire. The debasing institutions of the Aztecs furnish the best apology for their conquest. It is true, the conquerors brought along with them the Inquisition. But they also brought Christianity, whose benign radiance would still survive, when the fierce flames of fanaticism should be extinguished; dispelling those dark forms of horror which had so long brooded over the fair regions of Anahuac.

be rather said to ennoble him by devoting him to the gods. Although so terrible with the Aztecs, it was sometimes voluntarily embraced by them, as the most glorious death, and one that opened a sure passage into paradise. The Inquisition, on the other hand, branded its victims with infamy in this world, and consigned them to everlasting perdition in the next.

One detestable feature of the Aztec superstition, however, sunk it far below the Christian. This was its cannibalism; though, in truth, the Mexicans were not cannibals, in the coarsest acceptation of the term. They did

4 - Mexican hieroglyphics. - Manuscripts. - Arithmetic. - Chronology. - Astronomy.

It is a relief to turn from the gloomy pages of the preceding chapter, to a brighter side of the picture, and to contemplate the same nation in its generous struggle to raise itself from a nation of barbarism, and to take a positive rank in the scale of civilization. It is not the less interesting, that these efforts were made on an entirely new theatre of action, apart from those influences that operate in the Old World; the inhabitants of which, forming one great brotherhood of nations, are knit together by sympathies, that make the faintest spark of knowledge, struck out in one quarter, spread gradually wider, until it has diffused a cheering light over the remotest. It is curious to observe the human mind, in this new position, conforming to the same laws as on the ancient continent, and taking a similar direction in its first inquiries after truth,—so similar, indeed, as, although not warranting, perhaps, the idea of imitation, to suggest, at least, that of a common origin.

In the eastern hemisphere, we find some nations, as the Greeks, for instance, early smitten with such a love of the beautiful as to be unwilling to dispense with it, even in the graver productions of science, and other nations, again, proposing a severer end to themselves, to which even imagination and elegant art were made subservient. The productions of such a people must be criticized, not by the ordinary rules of taste, but by their adaptation to the peculiar end for which they were designed. Such were the Egyptians in the Old World, and the Mexicans in the New. We have already had occasion to notice the resemblance borne by the latter nation to the former in their religious economy. We

shall be more struck with it in their scientific culture, especially their hieroglyphical writings and their astronomy.

To describe actions and events by delineating visible objects seems to be a natural suggestion, and is practised, after a certain fashion, by the rudest savages. The North American Indian carves an arrow on the bark of trees to show his followers the direction of his march, and some other sign to show the success of his expeditions. But to paint intelligibly a consecutive series of these actions—forming what Warburton has happily called *picture-writing*—requires a combination of ideas, that amounts to a positively intellectual effort. Yet further, when the object of the painter, instead of being limited to the present, is, to penetrate the past, and to gather from its dark recesses lessons of instruction for coming generations, we see the dawnings of a literary culture,—and recognise the proof of a decided civilization in the attempt itself, however imperfectly it may be executed. The literal imitation of objects will not answer for this more complex and extended plan. It would occupy too much space, as well as time, in the execution. It then becomes necessary to abridge the pictures, to confine the drawing outlines, or to such prominent parts of the bodies delineated, as may readily suggest the whole. This is the *representative* or *figurative* writing, which forms the lowest stage of hieroglyphics.

But there are things which have no type in the material world; abstract ideas, which can only be represented by visible objects supposed to have some quality analogous to the idea intended. This constitutes *symbolical* writing, the most difficult of all to the interpreter, since the analogy between the material and immaterial object is often purely fanciful, or local in its application. Who, for instance, could suspect the association which made a beetle represent the universe, as with the Egyptians,

Detail of hieroglyphics on a stone at the angle of a pyramid at Monte Alban.

or a serpent typify time, as with the Aztecs?

The third and last division is the *phonetic,* in which signs are made to represent sounds, either entire words, or parts of them. This is the nearest approach of the hieroglyphical series to that beautiful invention, the alphabet, by which language is resolved into its elementary sounds, and an apparatus supplied for easily and accurately expressing the most delicate shades of thought.

The Egyptians were well skilled in all three kinds of hieroglyphics. But, although their public monuments display the first class, in their ordinary intercourse and written records, it is now certain, they almost wholly relied on the phonetic character. Strange, that, having thus broken down the thin partition which divided them from an alphabet, their latest monuments should exhibit no nearer approach to it than their earliest. The Aztecs, also, were acquainted with the several varieties of hieroglyphics. But they relied on the figurative infinitely more than on the others. The Egyptians were at the top of the scale, the Aztecs at the bottom.

In casting the eye over a Mexican manuscript, or map, as it is called, one is struck with the grotesque caricatures it exhibits of the human figure; monstrous, overgrown heads, on puny, misshapen bodies, which are themselves hard and angular in their outlines, and without the least skill in composition. On closer inspection, however, it is obvious that it is not so much a rude attempt to delineate nature, as a conventional symbol, to express the idea in the most clear and forcible manner; in the same way as the pieces of similar value on a chess-board, while they correspond with one another in form, bear little resemblance, usually, to the objects they represent. Those parts of the figure are most distinctly traced, which are the most important. So, also, the coloring, instead of the delicate gradations of nature, exhibits only gaudy and violent contrasts, such as may produce the most vivid impression. "For even colors", as Gama observes, "speak in the Aztec hieroglyphics".

But in the execution of all this the Mexicans were much inferior to the Egyptians. The drawings of the latter, indeed, are exceedingly defective, when criticised by the rules of art; for they were as ignorant of perspective as the Chinese, and only exhibited the head in profile, with the eye in the centre, and with total absence of expression. But they handled the pencil more gracefully than the Aztecs, were more true to the natural forms of objects, and, above all, showed great superiority in abridging the original figure by giving only the outline, or some characteristic or essential feature. This simplified the process, and facilitated the communication of thought. An Egyptian text has almost the appearance of alphabetical writing in its regular lines of minute figures. A Mexican text looks usually like a collection of pictures, each one forming the subject of a separate study. This is particularly the case with the delineations of mythology; in which the story is told by a conglomeration of symbols, that may remind one more of the mysterious anaglyphs sculptured on the temples of the Egyptians, than of their written records.

The Aztecs had various emblems for expressing such things as, from their nature, could not be directly represented by the painter; as, for example, the years, months, days, the seasons, the elements, the heavens, and the like. A "tongue" denoted speaking; a "foot-print", travelling; a "man sitting on

"The Aztecs were acquainted with the several varieties of hieroglyphics, but they relied on the figurative infinitely more than on the others".

the ground", an earthquake. These symbols were often very arbitrary, varying with the caprice of the writer; and it requires a nice discrimination to interpret them, as a slight change in the form or position of the figure intimated a very different meaning. An ingenious writer asserts that the priests devised secret symbolic characters for the record of their religious mysteries. It is possible. But the researches of Champollion lead to the conclusion, that the similar opinion, formerly entertained respecting the Egyptian hieroglyphics, is without foundation.

Lastly, they employed, as above stated, phonetic signs, though these were chiefly confined to the names of persons and places; which, being derived from some circumstance, or characteristic quality, were accommodated to the hieroglyphical system. Thus the town *Cimatlan* was compounded of *cimatl,* a "root, which grew near it, and *tlan,* signifying "near"; *Tlaxcallan* meant "the place of bread", from its rich fieds of corn; *Huexotzinco,* "a place surrounded by willows". The names of persons were often significant of their adventures and achievements. That of the great Tezcucan prince, Nezahualcoyotl, signified "hungry fox", intimating his sagacity, and his distresses in early life. The emblems of such names were no sooner seen, than they suggested to every Mexican the person and place intended; and, when painted on their shields, or embroidered on their banners, became the armorial bearings, by which city and chieftain were distinguished, as in Europe, in the age of chivalry.

But, although the Aztecs were instructed in all the varieties of hieroglyphical painting, they chiefly resorted to the clumsy method of direct representation. Had their empire lasted, like the Egyptian, several thousand, instead of the brief space of two hundred years, they would, doubtless, like them, have advanced to the more frequent use of the

65

phonetic writing. But, before they could be made acquainted with the capabilities of their own system, the Spanish Conquest, by introducing the European alphabet, supplied their scholars with a more perfect contrivance for expressing thought, which soon supplanted the ancient pictorial character.

Clumsy as it was, however, the Aztec picture-writing seems to have been adequate to the demands of the nation, in their imperfect state of civilization. By means of it were recorded all their laws, and even their regulations for domestic economy; their tribute-rolls, specifying the imposts of the various towns; their mythology, calendars, and rituals; their political annals, carried back to a period long before the foundation of the city. They digested a complete system of chronology, and could specify with accuracy the dates of the most important events in their history; the year being inscribed on the margin, against the particular circumstance recorded. It is true, history, thus executed, must necessarily be vague and fragmentary. Only a few leading incidents could be presented. But in this it did not differ much from the monkish chronicles of the dark ages, which often dispose of years in a few brief sentences; —quite long enough for the annals of barbarians.

In order to estimate aright the picture-writing of the Aztecs, one must regard it in connection with oral tradition, to which it was auxiliary. In the colleges of the priests the youth were instructed in astronomy, history, mythology, etc.; and those who were to follow the profession of hieroglyphical painting were taught the application of the characters appropriated to each of these branches. In an historical work, one had charge of the chronology, another of the events. Every part of the labor was thus mechanically distributed. The pupils, instructed in all that was before known in their

"Who could suspect the association which made a serpent typify time with the Aztecs?"

several departments, were prepared to extend still further the boundaries of their imperfect science. The hieroglyphics served as a sort of stenography, a collection of notes, suggesting to the initiated much more than could be conveyed by a literal interpretation. This combination of the written and the oral comprehended what may be called the literature of the Aztecs.

Their manuscripts were made of different materials,—of cotton cloth, or skins nicely prepared; of a composition of silk and gum; but, for the most part, of a fine fabric from the leaves of the aloe, *agave Americana,* called by the natives, *maguey,* which grows luxuriantly over the table-lands of Mexico. A sort of paper was made from it, resembling somewhat the Egyptian *papyrus,* which, when properly dressed and polished, is said to have been more soft and beautiful than parchment. Some of the specimens, still existing, exhibit their original freshness, and the paintings on them retain their brilliancy of colors. They were sometimes done up into rolls, but more frequently into volumes, of moderate size, in which the paper was shut up, like a folding-screen, with a leaf or tablet of wood at each extremity, that gave the whole, when closed, the appearance of a book. The length of the strips was determined only by convenience. As the pages might be read and referred to separately, this form had obvious advantages over the rolls of the ancients.

At the time of the arrival of the Spaniards, great quantities of these manuscripts were treasured up in the country. Numerous persons were employed in painting, and the dexterity of their operations excited the astonishment of the Conquerors. Unfortunately, this was mingled with other, and unworthy feelings. The strange, unknown characters inscribed on them excited suspicion. They were looked on as magic scrolls; and were regarded in the same light with the idols and temples, as the symbols of a pestilent superstition, that must be extirpated. The first archbishop of Mexico, Don Juan de Zumarraga,—a name that should be as immortal as that of Omar,—collected these paintings from every quarter, especially from Tezcuco, the most cultivated capital in Anahuac, and the great depository of the national archives. He then caused them to be piled up in a "mountain-heap",—as it is called by the Spanish writers themselves,—in the market-place of Tlatelolco, and reduced them all to ashes! His greater countryman, Archbishop Ximenes, had celebrated a similar *auto-da-fe* of Arabic manuscripts, in Granada, some twenty years before. Never did fana-ticism achieve two more signal triumphs, than by the annihilation of so many curious monuments of human ingenuity and learning!

The unlettered soldiers were not slow in imitating the example of their prelate. Every chart and volume which fell into their hands was wantonly destroyed; so that, when the scholars of a later and more enlightened age anxiously sought to recover some of these memorials of civilization, nearly all had perished, and the few surviving were jealously hidden by the natives. Through the indefatigable labors of a private individual, however, a considerable collection was eventually deposited in the archives of Mexico; but was so little heeded there, that some were plundered, others decayed piecemeal from the damps and mildews, and others, again, were used up as waste-paper! We contemplate with indignation the cruelties inflicted by the early conquerors. But indignation is qualified with contempt, when we see them thus ruthlessly trampling out the spark of knowledge, the common boon and property of all mankind. We may well doubt, which has the strongest claims to civilization, the victor, or the vanquished.

A few of the Mexican manuscripts have found their way, from time to time, to Europe, and are carefully preserved in the public libraries of its capitals. They are brought together in the magnificent work of Lord Kingsborough; but not one is there from Spain. The most important of them, for the light it throws on the Aztec institutions, is the Mendoza Codex; which, after its mysterious disappearance for more than a century, has at length·reappeared in the Bodleian library at Oxford. It has been several times engraved. The most brilliant in coloring, probably, is the Borgian collection, in Rome. The most curious, however, is the Dresden Codex, which has excited less attention than it deserves. Although usually classed among Mexican manuscripts, it bears little resemblance to them in its execution; the figures of objects are more delicately drawn, and the characters, unlike the Mexican, appear to be purely arbitrary, and are possibly phonetic. Their regular arrangement is quite equal to the Egyptian. The whole infers a much higher civilization than the Aztec, and offers abundant food for curious speculation.

Some few of these maps have interpretations annexed to them, which were obtained from the natives after the Conquest. The greater part are without any, and cannot now be unriddled. Had the Mexicans made free use of a phonetic alphabet, it might have been originally easy, by mastering the comparatively few signs employed in this kind of communication, to have got a permanent key to the whole. A brief inscription has furnished a clue to the vast labyrinth of Egyptian hieroglyphics. But the Aztec characters, representing individuals, or, at most, species, require to be made out separately; a hopeless task, for which little aid is to be expected from the vague and general tenor of the few interpretations now existing. There was, as already mentioned, until late in the last century, a professor in the University of Mexico, especially devoted to the study of the national picture-writing. But, as this was with a view to legal proceedings, his information, probably, was limited to deciphering title. In less than a hundred years after the Conquest, the knowledge of the hieroglyphics had so far declined, that a diligent Tezcucan writer complains he could find in the country only two persons, both very aged, at all competent to interpret them.

It is not probable, therefore, that the art of reading these picture-writings will ever be recovered; a circumstance certainly to be regretted. Not that the records of a semi-civilized people would be likely to contain any new truth or discovery important to

In this imposing site, the ruins of Monte Alban,
"the Acropolis of Mexico".

human comfort or progress; but they could scarcely fail to throw some additional light on the previous history of the nation, and that of the more polished people who before occupied the country. This would be still more probable, if any literary relics of their Toltec predecessors were preserved; and, if report be true, an important compilation from this source was extant at the time of the invasion, and may have perhaps contributed to swell the holocaust of Zumarraga. It is no great stretch of fancy, to suppose that such records might reveal the successive links in the mighty chain of migration of the primitive races, and, by carrying us back to the seat of their possessions in the Old World, have solved the mystery which has so long perplexed the learned, in regard to the settlement and civilization of the New.

Besides the hieroglyphical maps, the traditions of the country were embodied in the songs and hymns, which, as already mentioned, were carefully taught in the public schools. These were various, embracing the mythic legends of a heroic age, the warlike achievements of their own, or the softer tales of love and pleasure. Many of them were composed by scholars and persons of rank, and are cited as affording the most authentic record of events. The Mexican dialect was rich and expressive though inferior to the Tezcucan, the most polished of the idioms of Anahuac. None of the Aztec compositions have survived, but we can form some estimate of the general state of poetic culture from the odes which have come down to us from the royal house of Tezcuco. Sahagun has furnished us with translations of their more elaborate prose, consisting of prayers and public discourses, which give a favorable idea of their eloquence, and show that they paid much attention to rhetorical effect. They are said to have had, also, something like theatrical exhibitions, of a pantomimic sort, in which

A characteristic sculpture: such sculptures appeared at the lower part of the backs of the giants of Tula.

the faces of the performers were covered with masks, and the figures of birds or animals were frequently represented; an imitation, to which they may have been led by the familiar delineation of such objects in their hieroglyphics. In all this we see the dawning of a literary culture, surpassed, however, by their attainments in the severer walks of mathematical science.

They devised a system of notation in their arithmetic, sufficiently simple. The first twenty numbers were expressed by a corresponding number of dots. The first five had specific names; after which they were represented by combining the fifth with one of the four preceding; as five and one for six, five and two for seven, and so on. Ten and fifteen had each a separate name, which was also combined with the first four, to express a higher quantity. These four, therefore, were the radical characters of their oral arithmetic, in the same manner as they were of the written with the ancient Romans; a more simple arrangement, probably, than any existing among Europeans. Twenty was expressed by a separate hieroglyphic,—a flag. Larger sums were reckoned by twenties, and, in writing, by repeating the number of flags. The square of twenty, four hundred, had a separate sign, that of a plume, and so had the cube of twenty, or eight thousand, which was denoted by a purse, or sack. This was the whole arithmetical apparatus of the Mexicans, by the combination of which they were enabled to indicate any quantity. For greater expedition, they used to denote fractions of the larger sums by drawing only a part of the object. Thus, half or three fourths of a plume, or of a purse, represented that proportion of their respective sums, and so on. With all this, the machinery will appear very awkward to us, who perform our operations with so much ease, by means of the Arabic, or, rather, Indian ciphers. It is not much

"In the measurement of time, the Aztecs adjusted their civil year by the solar. They divided it into eighteen months of twenty days each".
—The hieroglyphics of the Mexican year.

more awkward, however, than the system pursued by the great mathematicians of antiquity, unacquainted with the brilliant invention, which has given a new aspect to mathematical science, of determining the value, in a great measure, by the relative position of the figures.

In the measurement of time, the Aztecs adjusted their civil year by the solar. They divided it into eighteen months of twenty days each. Both months and days were expressed by peculiar hieroglyphics,—those of the former often intimating the season of the year, like the French months, at the period of the Revolution. Five complementary days, as in Egypt, were added, to make up the full number of three hundred and sixty-five. They belonged to no month, and were regarded as peculiarly unlucky. A month was divided into four weeks, of five days each, on the last of which was the public fair, or market day. This arrangement, differing from that of the nations of the Old Continent, whether of Europe or Asia, has the advantage of giving an equal number

"A month was divided into four weeks, of five days each". Other hieroglyphics of the Mexican calendar.

of days to each month, and of comprehending entire weeks, without a fraction, both in the months and in the year.

As the year is composed of nearly six hours more than three hundred and sixty-five days, there still remained an excess, which, like other nations who have framed a calendar, they provided for by intercalation; not, indeed, every fourth year, as the Europeans, but at longer intervals, like some of the Asiatics. They waited till the expiration of fifty-two vague years, when they interposed thirteen days, or rather twelve and a half, this being the number which had fallen in arrear. Had they inserted thirteen, it would have been too much, since the annual excess over three hundred and sixty-five is about eleven minutes less than six hours. But, as their calendar, at the time of the Conquest, was found to correspond with the European, (making allowance for the subsequent Gregorian reform), they would seem to have adopted the shorter period of twelve days and a half, which brought them, within an almost inap-

preciable fraction, to the exact length of the tropical year, as established by the more accurate observations. Indeed, the intercalation of twenty-five days, in every hundred and four years, shows a nicer adjustment of civil to solar time than is presented by any European calendar; since more than five centuries must elapse, before the loss of an entire day. Such was the astonishing precision displayed by the Aztecs, or, perhaps, by their more polished Toltec predecessors, in these computations, so difficult as to have baffled, till a comparatively recent period, the most enlightened nations of Christendom!

The chronological system of the Mexicans, by which they determined the date of any particular event, was, also, very remarkable. The epoch, from which they reckoned, corresponded with the year 1091, of the Christian era. It was the period of the reform of their calendar, soon after their migration from Aztlan. They threw the years, as already noticed, into great cycles, of fifty-two each, which they called "sheafs", or "bundles" and represented by a quantity of reeds bound together by a string. As often as this hieroglyphic occurs in their maps, it shows the number of half centuries. To enable them to specify any particular year, they divided the great cycle into four smaller cycles, or indictions, of thirteen years each. They then adopted two periodical series of signs, one consisting of their numerical dots, up to thirteen, the other, of four hieroglyphics of the years. These latter they repeated in regular succession, setting against each one a number of the corresponding series of dots, continued also in regular succession up to thirteen. The same system was pursued through the four indictions, which thus, it will be observed, began always with a different hieroglyphic of the year from the preceding; and in this way, each of the hieroglyphics was made to combine successively with each of the numerical signs, but never twice with the same; since four, and thirteen, the factors of fifty-two,—the number of years in the cycle, —must admit of just as many combinations as are equal to their product. Thus every year had its appropriate symbol, by which it was, at once, recognised. And this symbol, preceded by the proper number of "bundles", indicating the half centuries, showed the precise time which had elapsed since the national epoch of 1091. The ingenious contrivance of a periodical series, in place of the cumbrous system of hieroglyphical notation, is not peculiar to the Aztecs, and is to be found among various people, on the Asiatic continent,—the same in principle, though varying materially in arrangement.

The solar calendar, above described, might have answered all the purposes of the nation; but the priests chose to construct another for themselves. This was called a "lunar reckoning", though nowise accommodated to the revolutions of the moon. It was formed, also, of two periodical series, one of them

74

An Aztec calendar (Museum of Mexico) and its "translation" in a picture of the last century.

consisting of thirteen numerical signs, or dots, the other, of the twenty hieroglyphics of the days. But, as the product of these combinations would only be 260, and, as some confusion might arise from the repetition of the same terms for the remaining 105 days of the years, they invented a third series, consisting of nine additional hieroglyphics, which, alternating with the two preceding series, rendered it impossible that the three should coincide twice in the same year, or indeed in less than 2340 days; since $20 \times 13 \times 9 = 2340$. Thirteen was a mystic number, of frequent use in their tables. Why they resorted to that of nine, on this occasion, is not so clear.

This second calendar rouses a holy indignation in the early Spanish missionaries, and father Sahagun loudly condemns it, as "most unhallowed, since it is founded neither on natural reason, nor on the influence of the planets, nor on the true course of the year; but is plainly the work of necromancy, and the fruit of a compact with the Devil!" One may doubt, whether the superstition of those who invented the scheme was greater than that of those who thus impugned it. At all events, we may, without having recourse to supernatural agency, find in the human heart a sufficient explanation of its origin; in that love of power, that has led the priesthood of many a faith to affect a mystery, the key to which was in their own keeping.

By means of this calendar, the Aztec priests kept their own records, regulated the festivals and seasons of sacrifice, and made all their astrological calculations. The false science of astrology is natural to a state of society partially civilized, where the mind, impatient of the slow and cautious examination by which alone it can arrive at truth, launches, at once, into the regions of speculation, and rashly attempts to lift the veil,—the impenetrable veil, which is drawn around the mysteries of nature. It is the characteristic of true science, to discern the impassable, but not very obvious, limits which divide the province of reason from that of speculation. Such knowledge comes tardily. How many ages have rolled away in which powers, that, rightly directed, might have revealed the great laws of nature, have been wasted in brilliant, but barren, reveries on alchemy and astrology!

The latter is more particularly the study of a primitive age; when the mind, incapable of arriving at the stupendous fact that the myriads of minute lights, glowing in the firmament, are the centres of systems as glorious as our own, is naturally led to speculate on their probable uses, and to connect them in some way or other with man, for whose convenience every other object in the universe seems to have been created. As the eye of the simple child of nature watches, through the long nights, the stately march of the heavenly bodies, and sees the bright hosts coming up, one after another, and changing with the changing seasons of the year, he naturally associates them with those seasons, as the periods over which they hold a mysterious influence. In the same manner, he connects their appearance with any interesting event of the time, and explores, in their flaming characters, the destinies of the new-born infant. Such is the origin of astrology, the false lights of which have continued from the earliest ages to dazzle and bewilder mankind, till they have faded away in the superior illumination of a comparatively recent period.

The astrological scheme of the Aztecs was founded less on the planetary influences, than on those of the arbitrary signs they had adopted for the months and days. The character of the leading sign, in each lunar cycle of thirteen days, gave a complexion to the whole; though this was qualified, in some degree, by the signs of the succeeding days, as well as by those of the hours. It was in adjusting these conflicting forces that the great art of the diviner was shown. In no country, not even in ancient Egypt, were the dreams of the astrologer more implicitly deferred to. On the birth of a child, he was instantly summoned. The time of the event was accurately ascertained; and the family hung in trembling suspense, as the minister of Heaven cast the horoscope of the infant, and unrolled the dark volume of destiny. The influence of the priest was confessed by the Mexican, in the very first breath which he inhaled.

We know little further of the astronomical attainments of the Aztecs. That they were acquainted with the cause of eclipses is evident from the representation, on their maps, of the disk of the moon projected on that of the sun. Whether they had arranged a system of constellations is uncertain; though, that they recognised some of the most obvious, as the Pleiades, for example, is evident from the fact that they regulated their festivals by them. We know of no astronomical instruments used by them, except the dial. An immense circular block of carved stone, disinterred in 1790, in the great square of Mexico, has supplied an acute and learned scholar with the means of establishing some interesting facts in regard to Mexican science. This colossal fragment, on which the calendar is engraved, shows that they had the means of settling the hours of the day with precision, the period of the solstices and of the equinoxes and that of the transit of the sun across the zenith of Mexico.

We cannot contemplate the astronomical science of the Mexicans, so disproportioned to their progress in other walks of civilization, without astonishment. An acquaintance with some of the more obvious principles of astronomy is within the reach of the rudest people. With a little care, they may learn to connect the regular changes of the seasons with those of the place of the sun at his rising and setting. They may follow the march of the great luminary through the heavens, by watching the stars that first brighten on his evening track, or fade in his morning beams. They may measure a revolution of the moon, by marking her phases, and may even form a general idea of the number of such revolutions in a solar year. But that they should be capable of accurately adjusting their festivals by the movements of the heavenly bodies, and should fix the true length of the tropical year, with a precision unknown to the great philosophers of antiquity, could be the result only of a long series of nice and patient observations, evincing no slight progress in civilization. But whence could the rude inhabitants of these mountain regions have derived this curious erudition? Not from the barbarous hordes who roamed over the higher latitudes of the North; nor from the more polished races on the Southern continent, with whom, it is apparent, they had no intercourse. If we are driven, in our embarrassment, like the greatest astronomer of our age, to seek the solution among the civilized communities of Asia, we shall still be perplexed by finding, amidst general resemblance of outline, sufficient discrepancy in the details, to vindicate, in the judgments of many, the Aztec claim to originality.

I shall conclude the account of Mexican science, with that of a remarkable festival, celebrated by the natives at the termination of the great cycle of fifty-two years. We have seen, in the preceding chapter, their tradition of the destruction of the world at four successive epochs. They looked forward confidently to another such catastrophe, to take place, like the preceding, at the close of a cycle, when the sun was to be effaced from the heavens, the human race, from the earth, and when the darkness of chaos was to settle on the habitable globe. The cycle would end in the latter part of December, and, as the dreary season of the winter solstice approached, and the diminished light of day gave melancholy presage of its speedy extinction, their apprehensions increased; and, on the arrival of the five "unlucky" days which closed the year, they abandoned themselves to despair. They broke in pieces the little images of their household gods, in whom they no longer trusted. The holy fires were suffered to go out in the temples, and none were lighted in their own dwellings. Their furniture and domestic utensils were destroyed; their garments torn in pieces; and every thing was thrown into disorder, for the coming of the evil genii who were to descend on the desolate earth.

On the evening of the last day, a procession of priests, assuming the dress and ornaments of their gods, moved from the capital towards a lofty mountain, about two leagues distant. They carried with them a noble victim, the flower of their captives, and an apparatus for kindling the *new fire,* the success of which was an augury of the renewal of the cycle. On reaching the summit of the mountain, the procession paused till midnight; when, as the constellation of the Pleiades approached the zenith, the *new fire* was kindled by the friction of the sticks placed on the wounded breast of the victim. The flame was soon communicated to a funeral pile, on which the body of the slaughtered captive was thrown. As the light streamed up towards heaven, shouts of joy and triumph burst forth from the countless multitudes who covered the hills, the terraces of the temples, and the house-tops, with eyes anxiously bent on the mount of sacrifice. Couriers, with torches lighted at the blazing beacon, rapidly bore them over every part of the country; and the cheering element was seen brightening on altar and hearth-stone, for the circuit of many

78

a league, long before the sun, rising on his accustomed track, gave assurance that a new cycle had commenced its march, and that the laws of nature were not to be reversed for the Aztecs.

The following thirteen days were given up to festivity. The houses were cleansed and whitened. The broken vessels were replaced by new ones. The people, dressed in their gayest apparel, and crowned with garlands and chaplets of flowers, thronged in joyous procession, to offer up their oblations and thanksgivings in the temples. Dances and games were instituted, emblematical of the regeneration of the world. It was the carnival of the Aztecs; or rather the national jubilee, the great secular festival, like that of the Romans, or ancient Etruscans, which few alive had witnessed before,—or could expect to see again.

An Observatory of ancient Mexico.

5 - Aztec Agriculture. - Mechanical Arts. - Merchants. - Domestic Manners.

It is hardly possible that a nation, so far advanced as the Aztecs in mathematical science, should not have made considerable progress in the mechanical arts, which are so nearly connected with it. Indeed, intellectual progress of any kind implies a degree of refinement, that requires a certain cultivation of both useful and elegant art. The savage, wandering through the wide forest, without shelter for his head, or raiment for his back, knows no other wants than those of animal appetites; and, when they are satisfied, seems to himself to have answered the only ends of existence. But man, in society, feels numerous desires, and artificial tastes spring up, accommodated to the various relations in which he is placed, and perpetually stimulating his invention to devise new expedients to gratify them.

There is a wide difference in the mechanical skill of different nations; but the difference is still greater in the inventive power which directs this skill, and makes it available. Some nations seem to have no power beyond that of imitation; or, if they possess invention, have it in so low a degree, that they are constantly repeating the same idea, without a shadow of alteration or improvement; as the bird builds precisely the same kind of nest which those of its own species built at the beginning of the world. Such, for example, are the Chinese, who have, probably, been familiar for ages with the germs of some discoveries, of little practical benefit to themselves, but which, under the influence of European genius, have reached a degree of excellence, that has wrought an important change in the constitution of society.

Far from looking back, and forming itself

Decorations on a house.

slavishly on the past, it is characteristic of the European intellect to be ever on the advance. Old discoveries become the basis of new ones. It passes onward from truth to truth, connecting the whole by a succession of links, as it were, into the great chain of science which is to encircle and bind together the universe. The light of learning is shed over the labors of art. New avenues are opened for the communication both of person and of thought. New facilities are devised for subsistence. Personal comforts, of every kind, are inconceivably multiplied, and brought within the reach of the poorest. Secure of these, the thoughts travel into a nobler region than that of the senses; and the appliances of art are made to minister to the demands of an elegant taste, and a higher moral culture.

The same enlightened spirit, applied to agriculture, raises it from a mere mechanical drudgery, or the barren formula of traditional precepts, to the dignity of a science. As the composition of the earth is analyzed, man learns the capacity of the soil that he cultivates; and, as his empire is gradually extended over the elements of nature, he gains the power to stimulate her to her most bountiful and various production. It is with satisfaction that we can turn to the land of our fathers, as the one in which the experiment has been conducted on the broadest scale, and attended with results that the world has never before witnessed. With equal truth, we may point to the Anglo-Saxon race in both hemispheres, as that whose enterprising genius has contributed most essentially to the great interests of humanity, by the application of science to the useful arts.

Husbandry, to a very limited extent, indeed, was practised by most of the rude tribes of North America. Whenever a natural opening in the forest, or a rich strip of *interval,* met their eyes, or a green slope was found along the rivers, they planted it with beans and Indian corn. The cultivation was slovenly in the extreme, and could not secure the improvident natives from the frequent recurrence of desolating famines. Still, that they tilled the soil at all was a peculiarity which honorably distinguished them from other tribes of hunters, and raised them one degree higher in the scale of civilization.

Agriculture in Mexico was in the same advanced state as the other arts of social life. In few countries, indeed, has it been more respected. It was closely interwoven with the civil and religious institutions of the nation. There were peculiar deities to preside over it; the names of the months and of the religious festivals had more or less reference to it. The public taxes, as we have seen, were often paid in agricultural produce. All, except the soldiers and great nobles, even the inhabitants of the cities, cultivated the soil. The work was chiefly done by the men; the women scattering the

seed, husking the corn, and taking part only in the lighter labors of the field. In this they presented an honorable contrast to the other tribes of the continent, who imposed the burden of agriculture, severe as it is in the North, on their women. Indeed, the sex was as tenderly regarded by the Aztecs in this matter, as it is, in most parts of Europe, at the present, day.

There was no want of judgment in the management of their ground. When somewhat exhausted, it was permitted to recover by lying fallow. Its extreme dryness was relieved by canals, with which the land was partially irrigated; and the same end was promoted by severe penalties against the destruction of the woods, with which the country, as already noticed, was well covered before the Conquest. Lastly, they provided for their harvests ample granaries, which were admitted by the Conquerors to be of admirable construction. In the provision we see the forecast of civilized man.

Among the most important articles of husbandry, we may notice the banana, whose facility of cultivation and exuberant returns are so fatal to habits of systematic and hardy industry. Another celebrated plant was the cacao, the fruit of which furnished the chocolate,—from the Mexican *chocolatl,*—now so common a beverage throughout Europe. The vanilla, confined to a small district of the seacoast, was used for the same purposes, of flavoring their food and drink, as with us. The great staple of the country, as, indeed, of the American continent, was maize, or Indian corn, which grew freely along the valleys, and up the steep sides of the Cordilleras to the high level of the table-land. The Aztecs were as curious in its preparation, and as well instructed in its

"The great staple of the country was maize, or Indian corn". A Codex shows the maize being cultivated and gathered; the statuette opposite presents a woman grinding the ears. Right: plantation of papaias.

The ancient Mexicans, husbandmen, were much concerned with the rains. Above: a pluviometer. Below and right: god (Tlaloc) and goddess of the Rain.

manifold uses, as the most expert New England housewife. Its gigantic stalks, in these equinoctial regions, afford a saccharine matter, not found to the same extent in northern latitudes, and supplied the natives with sugar little inferior to that of the cane itself, which was not introduced among them till after the Conquest. But the miracle of nature was the great Mexican aloe, or *maguey,* whose clustering pyramids of flowers, towering above their dark coronals of leaves, were seen sprinkled over many a broad acre of the table-land. As we have already noticed its bruised leaves afforded a paste from which paper was manufactured; its juice was fermented into an intoxicating beverage, *pulque,* of which the natives, to this day, are excessively fond; its leaves further supplied an impenetrable thatch for the more humble dwellings; thread, of which coarse stuffs were made, and strong cords, were drawn from its tough and twisted fibres; pins and needles were made of the thorns at the extremity of its leaves; and the root, when properly cooked, was converted into a palatable and nutritious food. The *agave,* in short, was meat, drink, clothing, and writing materials, for the Aztecs ! Surely, never did Nature enclose in so compact a form

"The opposite climates embraced within the narrow latitudes of New Spain have given to it, probably, the richest and most diversified Flora to be found in any country on the globe".

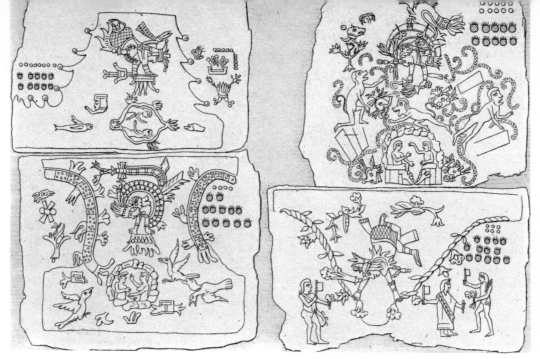

Representation of the seasons by the Aztecs, on bas-relief.

so many of the elements of human comfort and civilization !

It would be obviously out of place to enumerate in these pages all the varieties of plants, many of them of medicinal virtue, which have been introduced from Mexico into Europe. Still less can I attempt a catalogue of its flowers, which, with their variegated and gaudy colors, form the greatest attraction of our greenhouses. The opposite climates embraced within the narrow latitudes of New Spain have given to it, probably, the richest and most diversified Flora to be found in any country on the globe. These different products were systematically arranged by the Aztecs, who understood their properties, and collected them into nurseries, more extensive than any then existing in the Old World. It is not improbable that they suggested the idea of those "gardens of plants" which were introduced into Europe not many years after the Conquest.

The Mexicans were as well acquainted with the mineral, as with the vegetable treasures of their kingdom. Silver, lead, and tin they drew from the mines of Tasco, copper from the mountains of Zacotollan. These were taken, not only from the crude masses on the surface, but from veins wrought in the solid rock, into which they opened extensive galleries. In fact, the traces of their labors furnished the best indications for the early Spanish miners. Gold, found on the surface, or gleaned from the beds of rivers, was cast into bars, or, in the form of dust, made parts of the regular tribute of the southern provinces of the empire. The use of iron, with which the soil was impregnated, was unknown to them. Notwithstanding its abundance, it demands so many processes to prepare it for use, that it has commonly been one of the last metals pressed into the service of man. The age of iron has followed that of brass, in fact as well as in fiction.

They found a substitute in an alloy of tin

and copper; and, with tools made of this bronze, could cut not only metals, but, with the aid of a silicious dust, the hardest substances, as basalt, porphyry, amethysts, and emeralds. They fashioned these last, which were found very large, into many curious and fantastic forms. They cast, also, vessels of gold and silver, carving them with their metallic chisels in a very delicate manner. Some of the silver vases were so large that a man could not encircle them with his arms. They imitated very nicely the figures of animals, and, what was extraordinary, could mix the metals in such a manner, that the feathers of a bird, or the scales of a fish, should be alternately of gold and silver. The Spanish goldsmiths admitted their superiority over themselves in these ingenious works.

They employed another tool, made of *itztli*, or obsidian, a dark transparent mineral, exceedingly hard, found in abundance in their hills. They made it into knives, razors, and their serrated swords. It took a keen edge, though soon blunted. With this they wrought the various stones and alabasters employed in the construction of their public works and principal dwellings. I shall defer a more particular account of these to the body of the narrative, and will only add here, that the entrances and angles of the buildings were profusely ornamented with images, sometimes of their fantastic deities, and frequently of animals. The latter were executed with great accuracy. "The former," according to Torquemada, "were the hideous reflection of their own souls. And it was not till after they had been converted to Christianity, that they could model the true figure of a man." The old chronicler's facts are well founded, whatever we may think of his reasons. The allegorical phantasms of his religion, no doubt, gave a direction to the Aztec artist, in his delineation of the human figure; supplying him with an imaginary beauty in the personification of divinity

Remains of a palace: an elaborate architecture.

itself. As these superstitions lost their hold on his mind, it opened to the influences of a purer taste; and after the Conquest, the Mexicans furnished many examples of correct, and some of beautiful portraiture.

Sculptured images were so numerous, that foundations of the cathedral in the *plaza mayor,* the great square of Mexico, are said to be entirely composed of them. This spot may, indeed, be regarded as the Aztec forum,—the great depository of the treasures of ancient sculpture, which now lie hid in its bosom. Such monuments are spread all over the capital, however, and a new cellar can hardly be dug, or foundation laid, without turning up some of the mouldering relics of barbaric art. But they are little heeded, and, if not wantonly broken in pieces at once, are usually worked into the rising wall, or supports of the new edifice. Two celebrated bas-reliefs, of the last Montezuma and his father, cut in the solid rock, in the beautiful groves of Chapoltepec, were deliberately destroyed, as late as the last century, by order of the governement ! The monuments of the barbarian meet with as little respect from civilized man, as those of the civilized man from the barbarian.

The most remarkable piece of sculpture yet disinterred is the great calendar-stone, noticed in the preceding chapter. It consists of dark porphyry, and, in its original dimensions, as taken from the quarry, is computed to have weighed nearly fifty tons. It was transported from the mountains beyond Lake Chalco, a distance of many leagues, over a broken country intersected by water-courses and canals. In crossing a bridge which traversed one of these latter, in the capital, the support gave way and the huge mass was precipitated into the water, whence it was with difficulty recovered. The fact, that so enormous a fragment of porphyry could be thus safely carried for leagues, in the face of such obstacles, and without the aid of cattle,—for the

Remains of a temple at Mitla.

Aztecs, as already mentioned, had no animals of draught,—suggests to us no mean ideas of their mechanical skill, and of their machinery; and implies a degree of cultivation, little inferior to that demanded for the geometrical and astronomical science displayed in the inscriptions on this very stone.

The ancient Mexicans made utensils of earthen ware for the ordinary purposes of domestic life, numerous specimens of which still exist. They made cups and vases of a lackered or painted wood, impervious to wet and gaudily colored. Their dyes were obtained from both mineral and vegetable substances. Among them was the rich crimson of the cochineal, the modern rival of the famed Tyrian purple. It was introduced into Europe from Mexico, where the curious little insect was nourished with great care on plantations of cactus, since fallen into neglect. The natives were thus enabled to give a brilliant coloring to the webs, which were manufactured of every degree of fineness, from the cotton raised in abundance throughout the warmer regions of the country. They had the art, also, of interweaving with these the delicate hair of rabbits and other animals, which made a cloth of great warmth as well as beauty, of a kind altogether original; and on this they often laid a rich embroidery, of birds, flowers, or some other fanciful device.

But the art in which they most delighted was their *plumaje,* or featherwork. With this they could produce all the effect of a beautiful mosaic. The gorgeous plumage of the tropical birds, especially of the parrot tribe, afforded every variety of color; and the fine down of the humming-bird, which revelled in swarms among the honeysuckle bowers of Mexico, supplied them with soft aërial tints that gave an exquisite finish to the picture. The feathers, pasted on a fine cotton web, were wrought into dresses for the wealthy, hangings for apartments, and

ornaments for the temples. No one of the American fabrics excited such admiration in Europe, whither numerous specimens were sent by the Conquerors. It is to be regretted, that so graceful an art should have been suffered to fall into decay.

There were no shops in Mexico, but the various manufactures and agricultural products were brought together for sale in the great market-places of the principal cities. Fairs were held there every fifth day, and were thronged by a numerous concourse of persons, who came to buy or sell from all the neighbouring country. A particular quarter was allotted to each kind of article. The numerous transactions were conducted without confusion, and with entire regard to justice, under the inspection of magistrates appointed for the purpose. The traffic was carried on partly by barter, and partly by means of a regulated currency, of different values. This consited of transparent quills of gold dust; of bits of tin, cut in the form of a T and of bags of cacao, containing a specified number of grains. "Blessed money" exclaims Peter Martyr, "which exempts its possessors from avarice, since it cannot be long hoarded, nor hidden under ground !"

There did not exist in Mexico that distinction of castes found among the Egyptian and Asiatic nations. It was usual, however, for the son to follow the occupation of his father. The different trades were arranged into something like guilds; having, each, a particular district of the city appropriated to it, with its own chief, its own tutelar deity, its peculiar

"The Aztec merchant carried with him merchandise of rich stuff."
Above: two itinerant merchants.

held for the sale of these unfortunate beings. They were brought thither by their masters, dressed in their gayest apparel, and instructed to sing, dance, and display their little stock of personal accomplishments, so as to recommend themselves to the purchaser. Slave-dealing was an honorable calling among the Aztec.

With this rich freight, the merchant visited the different provinces, always bearing some

This statuette represents a porter.

festivals, and the like. Trade was held in avowed estimation by the Aztecs. "Apply thyself, my son", was the advice of an aged chief, "to agriculture, or to feather-work, or some other honorable calling. Thus did your ancestors before you. Else, how would they have provided for themselves and their families? Never was it heard, that nobility alone was able to maintain its possessor." Shrewd maxims, that must have sounded somewhat strange in the ear of a Spanish *hidalgo* !

But the occupation peculiarly respected was that of the merchant. It formed so important and singular a feature of their social economy, as to merit a much more particular notice than it has received from historians. The Aztec merchant was a sort of itinerant trader, who made his journeys to the remotest borders of Anahuac, and to the countries beyond, carrying with him merchandise of rich stuffs, jewelry, slaves, and other valuable commodities. The slaves were obtained at the great market of Azcapozalco, not many leagues from the capital, where fairs were regularly

92

present of value from his own sovereign to the chiefs, and usually receiving others in return, with a permission to trade. Should this be denied him, or should he meet with indignity or violence, he had the means of resistance in his power. He performed his journeys with a number of companions of his own rank, and a large body of inferior attendants who were employed to transport the goods. Fifty or sixty pounds were the usual load for a man.

The whole caravan went armed, and so well provided against sudden hostilities, that they could make good their defence, if necessary, till reinforced from home. In one instance, a body of these militant traders stood a siege of four years in the town of Ayotlan which they finally took from the enemy. Their own government, however, was always prompt to embark in a war on this ground, finding it a very convenient pretext for extending the

"The various manufactures and agricultural products were brought together for sale in the great market-places of the principal cities". Remains of such a market.

Mexican empire. It was not unusual to allow the merchants to raise levies themselves, which were placed under their command. It was, moreover, very common for the prince to employ the merchants as a sort of spies, to furnish him information of the state of the countries through which they passed, and the dispositions of the inhabitants towards himself.

Thus their sphere of action was much enlarged beyond that of a humble trader, and they acquired a high consideration in the body politic. They were allowed to assume insignia and devices of their own. Some of their number composed what is called by the Spanish writers a council of finance; at least, this was the case in Tezcuco. They were much consulted by the monarch, who had some of them constantly near his person; addressing them by the title of "uncle", which may remind one of that of *primo,* or "cousin," by which a grandee of Spain is saluted by his sovereign. They were allowed to have their own courts, in which civil and criminal cases, not excepting capital, were determined; so that they formed an independent community, as it were, of themselves. And, as their various traffic supplied them with abundant stores of wealth, they enjoyed many of the most essential advantages of an hereditary aristocracy.

That trade should prove the path of eminent political preferment in a nation but partially civilized, where the names of soldier and priest are usually the only titles to respect, is certainly an anomaly in history. It forms some contrast to the standard of the more polished monarchies of the Old World, in which rank is supposed to be less dishonored by a life of idle ease or frivolous pleasure, than by those active pursuits which promote equally the prosperity of the state and of the individual. If civilization corrects many prejudices, it must be allowed that it creates others.

We shall be able to form a better idea of the actual refinement of the natives, by penetrating

Left: Coatlicue, goddess of the earth, life and death.
Right: the god of virility... in ecstasy.

into their domestic life and observing the intercourse between the sexes. We have fortunately the means of doing this. We shall there find the ferocious Aztec frequently displaying all the sensibility of a cultivated nature; consoling his friends under affliction, or congratulating them on their good fortune, as on occasion of a marriage, or of the birth or the baptism of a child, when he was punctilious in his visits, bringing presents of costly dresses and ornaments, or the more simple offering of flowers,

This statuette of a naked child crying dates back to the pre-Aztec civilization.—Right: wedding and birth, in a Codex.

equally indicative of his sympathy. The visits, at these times, though regulated with all the precision of Oriental courtesy, were accompanied by expressions of the most cordial and affectionate regard.

The discipline of children, especially at the public schools, as stated in a previous chapter, was exceedingly severe. But after she had come to a mature age, the Aztec maiden was treated by her parents with a tenderness, from which all reserve seemed banished. In the counsels to a daughter about to enter into life, they conjured her to preserve simplicity in her manners and conversation, uniform neatness in her attire, with strict attention to personal cleanliness. They inculcated modesty, as the great ornament of a woman, and implicit reverence for her husband; softening their admonitions by such endearing epithets, as showed the fulness of a parent's love.

Polygamy was permitted among the Mexicans, though chiefly confined, probably, to the wealthiest classes. And the obligations of the marriage vow, which was made with all the formality of a religious ceremony, were fully recognised, and impressed on both parties. The women are described by the Spaniards as pretty, unlike their infortunate descendants, of the present day, though with the same serious and rather melancholy cast of countenance. Their long black hair, covered, in some parts of the country, by a veil made of the fine web of the *pita,* might generally be seen wreathed with flowers, or, among the richer people, with strings of precious stones, and pearls from the Gulf of California. They appear to have been treated with much consideration by their husbands; and passed their time in indolent tranquillity, or in such feminine occupations as spinning, embroidery, and the like; while their maidens beguiled the hours by the rehearsal of traditionary tales and ballads.

The women partook equally with the men of social festivities and entertainments. These

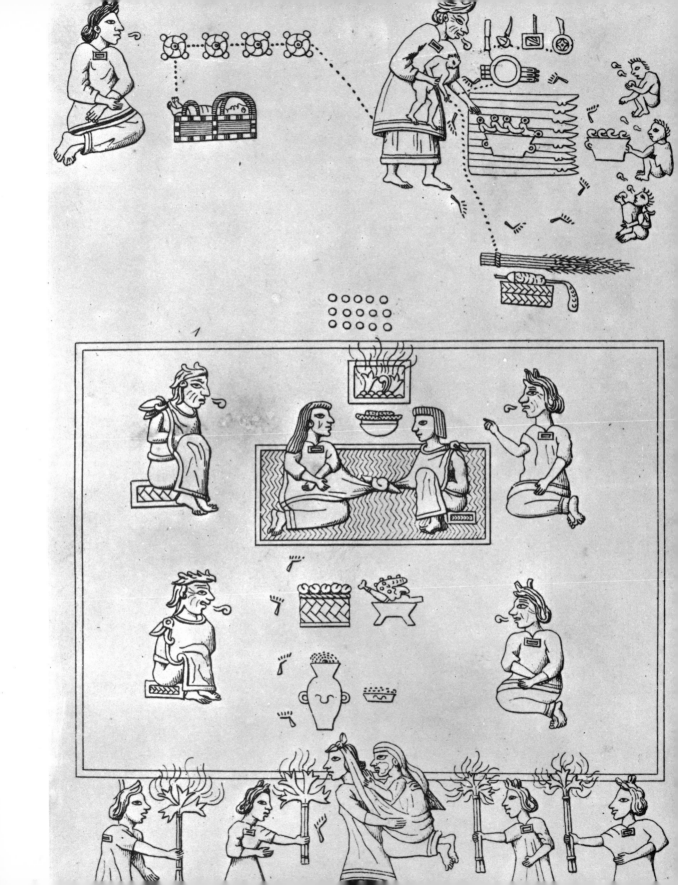

were often conducted on a large scale, both as regards the number of guests and the costliness of the preparations. Numerous attendants, of both sexes, waited at the banquet. The halls were scented with perfumes, and the courts strewed with odoriferous herbs and flowers, which were distributed in profusion among the guests, as they arrived. Cotton napkins and ewers of water were placed before them, as they took their seats at the board; for the venerable ceremony of ablution, before and after eating, was punctiliously observed by the Aztecs. Tobacco was then offered to the company, in pipes, mixed up with aromatic substances, or in the form of cigars, inserted in tubes of tortoise-shell or silver. They compressed the nostrils with the fingers, while they inhaled the smoke, which they frequently swallowed. Whether the women, who sat apart from the men at table, were allowed the indulgence of the fragrant weed, as in the most polished circles of modern Mexico, is not told

us. It is a curious fact, that the Aztecs also took the dried leaf in the pulverized form of snuff.

The table was well provided with substantial meats, especially game; among which the most conspicuous was the turkey, erroneously supposed, as its name imports, to have come originally from the East. These more solid dishes were flanked by others of vegetables and fruits, of every delicious variety found on the North American continent. The different viands were prepared in various ways, with delicate sauces and seasoning, of which the Mexicans were very fond. Their palate was still further regaled by confections and pastry, for which their maizeflour and sugar supplied ample materials. One other dish, of a disgusting nature, was sometimes added to the feast, especially when the celebration partook of a religious character. On such occasions a slave was sacrificed, and his flesh, elaborately dressed, formed one of the chief ornaments of the banquet. Cannibalism, in the guise of an Epicurean science, becomes even revolting.

The meats were kept warm by chafing-dishes. The table was ornamented with vases of silver, and sometimes gold, of delicate workmanship. The drinking cups and spoons were of the same costly materials, and likewise of tortoise shell. The favorite beverage was the *chocolatl,* flavored with vanilla and different spices. They had a way of preparing the froth of it, so as to make it almost solid enough to be eaten, and took it cold. The fermented juice of the maguey, with a mixture of sweets and acids, supplied, also, various agreeable drinks, of different degrees of strength, and formed the chief beverage of the elder part of the company.

As soon as they had finished their repast, the young people rose from the table, to close the festivities of the day with dancing. They danced gracefully, to the sound of various instruments, accompanying their movements with chants, of a pleasing, though somewhat plaintive character. The older guests continued at table, sipping *pulque,* and gossiping about other times, till the virtues of the exhilarating beverage put them in good-humor with their own. Intoxication was not rare in this part of the company, and, what is singular, was excused in them, though severely punished in the younger. The entertainment was concluded by a liberal distribution of rich dresses and ornaments among the guests, when they

"The Aztecs danced gracefully, to the sound of various instruments". Below, a pelota player. —"Human nature is, indeed, much the same all over the world"...

withdrew, after midnight, "some commending the feast, and others condemning the bad taste or extravagance of their host, in the same manner", says an old Spanish writer, "as with us". Human nature is, indeed, much the same all the world over.

In this remarkable picture of manners, which I have copied faithfully from the records of earliest date after the Conquest, we find no resemblance to the other races of North American Indians. Some resemblance we may trace to the general style of Asiatic pomp and luxury. But, in Asia, woman, far from being admitted to unreserved intercourse with the other sex, is too often jealously immured within the walls of the harem. European civilization, which accords to this loveliest portion of creation her proper rank in the social scale, is still more removed from some of the brutish usages of the Aztecs. That such usages should have existed with the degree of refinement they showed in other things is almost inconceivable. It can only be explained as the result of religious superstition; superstition which clouds the moral perception, and perverts even the natural senses, till man, civilized man, is reconciled to the very things which are most revolting to humanity. Habits and opinions founded on religion must not be taken as conclusive evidence of the actual refinement of a people.

The Aztec character was perfectly original and unique. It was made up of incongruities apparently irreconcilable. It blended into one the marked peculiarities of different nations, not only of the same phase of civilization, but as far removed from each other as the extremes of barbarism and refinement. It may find a fitting parallel in their own wonderful climate, capable of producing, on a few square leagues of surface, the boundless variety of vegetable forms, which belong to the frozen regions of the North, the temperate zone of Europe, and the burning skies of Arabia and Hindostan!

This naive picture represents a Turkish bath; the photo opposite shows the remains of hot baths. Opposite: terra-cotta evoking hairdressing. Right: remains of a house called "the house of the phallus".

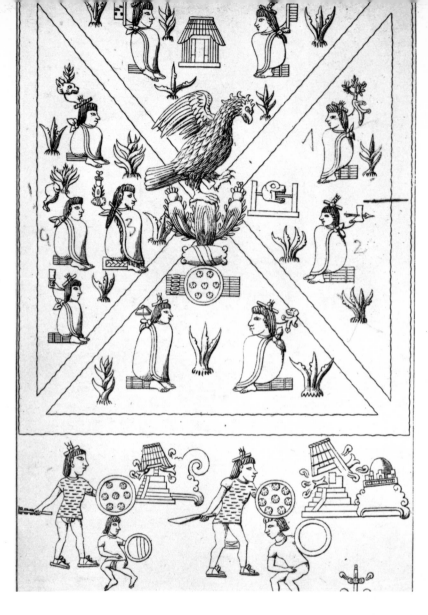

Mexico:—an Aztec representation ("The legend of its foundation is still further commemorated by the device of the eagle and the cactus")—a reconstitution ordered- perhaps by Cortes- at the time of the Spanish conquest; —then a little later, with a view of the site;—and then an eighteenth century picture, executed from the informations of ancient historians.

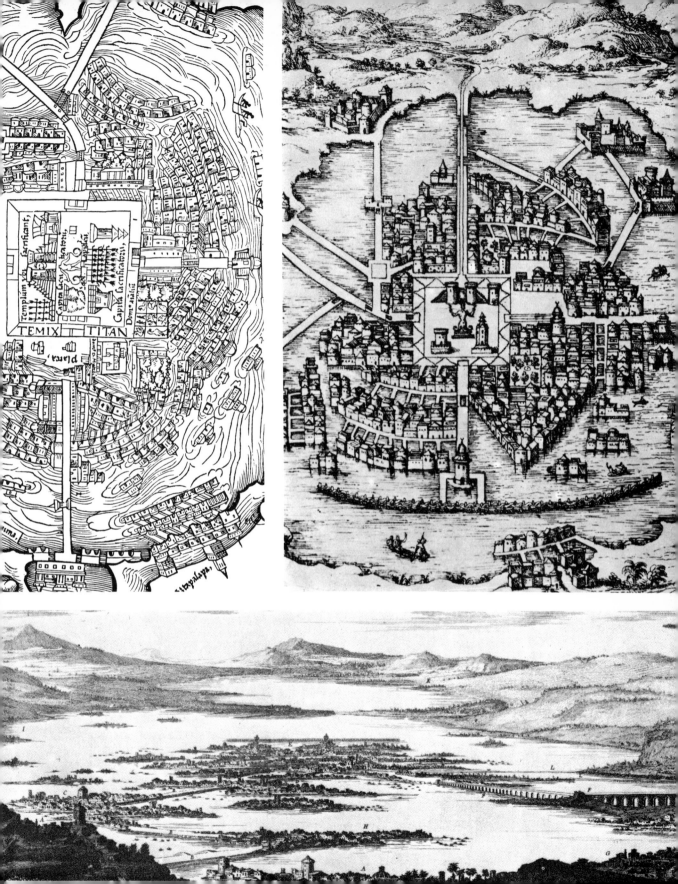

TEMIX TITAN

Templum in facrificant,
Capita locis fratotii,
capita
Capita facrificatorii,
Domi aualis

Plaza,

We can see here a funeral urn and the figure it presents is the more curious as it is... the god of Joy.

6 - Tezcucans. - Their golden age. - Accomplished princes. - Decline of their monarchy.

The reader would gather but an imperfect notion of the civilization of Anahuac, without some account of the Acolhuans, or Tezcucans, as they are usually called; a nation of the same great family with the Aztecs, whom they rivalled in power, and surpassed in intellectual culture and the arts of social refinement. Fortunately, we have ample materials for this in the records left by Ixtlilxochitl, a lineal descendant of the royal line of Tezcuco, who flourished in the century of the Conquest. With every opportunity for information he combined much industry and talent, and, if his narrative bears the high coloring of one who would revive the faded glories of an ancient, but dilapidated house, he has been uniformly commended for his fairness and integrity, and has been followed without misgiving by such Spanish writers as could have access to his manuscripts. I shall confine myself to the prominent features of the two reigns which may be said to embrace the golden age of Tezcuco; without attempting to weigh the probability of the details, which I will leave to be settled by the reader, according to the measure of his faith.

The Acolhuans came into the Valley, as we have seen, about the close of the twelfth century, and built their capital of Tezcuco on the eastern borders of the lake, opposite to Mexico. From this point they gradually spread themselves over the northern portion of Anahuac, when their career was checked by an invasion of a kindred race, the Tepanecs, who, after a desperate struggle, succeeded in taking their city, slaying their monarch, and entirely subjugating his kingdom. This event took place about 1418; and the young prince, Nezahualcoyotl, the heir to the crown, then fifteen years old, saw his father butchered before his eyes, while he himself lay concealed among the friendly branches of a tree, which overshadowed the spot. His subsequent history is as full of romantic daring, and perilous escapes, as that of the renowned Scanderbeg, or of the "young Chevalier".

Not long after his flight from the field of his father's blood, the Tezcucan prince fell into the hands of his enemy, was borne off in triumph to his city, and was thrown into a dungeon. He effected his escape, however, through the connivance of the governor of the fortress, an old servant of his family, who took the place of the royal fugitive, and paid for his loyalty with his life. He was at length permitted, through the intercession of the reigning family in Mexico, which was allied to him, to retire to that capital, and subsequently to his own, where he found a shelter in his ancestral palace. Here he remained unmolested for eight years, pursuing his studies under an old preceptor, who had had the care of his early youth, and who instructed him in the various duties befitting his princely station.

At the end of this period the Tepanec usurper died, bequeathing his empire to his son, Maxtla, a man of fierce and suspicious temper. Nezahualcoyotl hastened to pay his obeisance to him, on his accession. But the tyrant refused to receive the little present of flowers which he laid at his feet, and turned his back on him in presence of his chieftains. One of his attendants, friendly to the young prince, admonished him to provide for his own safety, by withdrawing, as speedily as possible, from the palace, where his life was in danger. He lost no time, consequently, in retreating from the inhospitable court, and returned to Tezcuco. Maxtla, however, was bent on his destruction. He saw with jealous eye the opening talents and popular manners

105

of his rival, and the favor he was daily winning from his ancient subjects.

He accordingly laid a plan for making way with him at an evening entertainment. It was defeated by the vigilance of the prince's tutor, who contrived to mislead the assassins, and to substitute another victim in the place of his pupil. The baffled tyrant now threw off all disguise, and sent a strong party of soldiers to Tezcuco, with orders to enter the palace, seize the person of Nezahualcoyotl, and slay him on the spot. The prince, who became acquainted with the plot through the watchfulness of his preceptor, instead of flying, as he was counselled, resolved to await his enemy. They found him playing at ball, when they arrived, in the court of his palace. He received them courteously, and invited them in, to take some refreshments after their journey. While they were occupied in this way, he passed into an adjoining saloon, which excited no suspicion, as he was still visible through the open doors by which the apartments communicated with each other. A burning censer stood in the passage, and, as it was fed by the attendants, threw up such clouds of incense as obscured his movements from the soldiers. Under this friendly veil he succeeded in making his escape by a secret passage, which communicated with a large earthen pipe formerly used to bring water to the palace. Here he remained till night-fall, when, taking advantage of the obscurity, he found his way into the suburbs, and sought a shelter in the cottage of one of his father's vassals.

The Tepanec monarch, enraged at this repeated disappointment, ordered instant pursuit. A price was set on the head of the royal fugitive. Whoever should take him, dead or alive, was promised, however humble his degree, the hand of a noble lady, and an ample domain along with it. Troops of armed men were ordered to scour the country in every direction. In the course of the search, the cottage, in which the prince had taken refuge, was entered. But he fortunately escaped detection by being hid under a heap of maguey fibres used for manufacturing cloth. As this was no longer a proper place of concealment, he sought a retreat in the mountainous and woody district lying between the borders of his own state and Tlascala.

Here he led a wretched, wandering life, exposed to all the inclemencies of the weather, hiding himself in deep thickets and caverns, and stealing out, at night, to satisfy the cravings of appetite; while he was kept in constant alarm by the activity of his pursuers, always hovering on his track. On one occasion he sought refuge from them among a small party of soldiers, who proved friendly to him, and concealed him in a large drum around which they were dancing. At another time, he was just able to turn the crest of a hill, as his enemies were climbing it on the other side, when he fell in with a girl who was reaping *chian*,—a Mexican plant, the seed of which was much used in the drinks of the country. He persuaded her to cover him up with the stalks she had been cutting. When his pursuers came up, and inquired if she had seen the fugitive, the girl coolly answered that she had, and pointed out a path as the one he had taken. Notwithstanding the high rewards offered, Nezahualcoyotl seems to have incurred no danger from treachery, such was the general attachment felt to himself and his house. "Would you not deliver up the prince, if he came in your way?" he inquired of a young peasant who was unacquainted with his person. "Not I", replied the other. "What, not for a fair lady's hand, and a rich dowry beside?" rejoined the prince. At which the other only shook his head and laughed. On more than one occasion, his faithful people submitted to torture, and even

*Another funeral urn, very old: here it is the
goddess of the Earth.*

to lose their lives, rather than disclose the place of his retreat.

However gratifying such proofs of loyalty might be to his feelings, the situation of the prince in these mountain solitudes became every day more distressing. It gave a still keener edge to his own sufferings to witness those of the faithful followers who chose to accompany him in his wanderings. "Leave me", he would say to them, "to my fate! Why should you throw away your own lives for one whom fortune is never weary of persecuting?" Most of the great Tezcucan chiefs had consulted their interests by a timely adhesion to the usurper. But some still clung to their prince, preferring proscription, and death itself, rather than desert him in his extremity.

In the mean time, his friends at a distance were active in measures for his relief. The oppressions of Maxtla, and his growing empire, had caused general alarm in the surrounding states, who recalled the mild rule of the Tezcucan princes. A coalition was formed, a plan of operations concerted, and, on the day appointed for a general rising, Nezahualcoyotl found himself at the head of a force sufficiently strong to face his Tepanec adversaries. An engagement came on, in which the latter were totally discomfited; and the victorious prince, receiving everywhere on his route the homage of his joyful subjects, entered his capital, not like a proscribed outcast, but as the rightful heir, and saw himself once more enthroned in the halls of his fathers.

Soon after, he united his forces with the Mexicans, long disgusted with the arbitrary conduct of Maxtla. The allied powers, after a series of bloody engagements with the usurper, routed him under the walls of his own capital. He fled to the baths, whence he was dragged out, and sacrificed with the usual cruel ceremonies of the Aztecs; the royal city of Azcapozalco was razed to the ground, and the wasted territory was henceforth reserved as the great slave-market for the nations of Anahuac.

These events were succeeded by the remarkable league among the three powers of Tezcuco, Mexico, and Tlacopan, of which some account has been given in a previous chapter. Historians are not agreed as to the precise terms of it; the writers of the two former nations, each, insisting on the paramount authority of his own in the coalition. All agree in the subordinate position of Tlacopan, a state, like the others, bordering on the lake. It is certain, that in their subsequent operations, whether of peace or war, the three states shared in each other's councils, embarked in each other's enterprises, and moved in perfect concert together till just before the coming of the Spaniards.

The first measure of Nezahualcoyotl, on returning to his dominions was a general amnesty. It was his maxim, "that a monarch might punish, but revenge was unworthy of him". In the present instance, he was averse even to punish, and not only freely pardoned his rebel nobles, but conferred on some, who had most deeply offended, posts of honor and confidence. Such conduct was doubtless politic, especially as their alienation was owing, probably, much more to fear of the usurper, than to any disaffection towards himself. But there are some acts of policy which a magnanimous spirit only can execute.

The restored monarch next set about repairing the damages sustained under the late misrule, and reviving, or rather remodelling, the various departments of government. He framed a concise, but comprehensive, code of laws, so well suited, it was thought to the exigencies of the times, that it was adopted as their own by the two other members of the triple alliance. It was written in blood, and entitled the author to be called the Draco, rather than "the Solon of Anahuac", as he is fondly styled by his admirers. Humanity is one of the best fruits of refinement. It is only with increasing civilization that the legislator studies to economize human suffering, even for the guilty; to devise penalties, not so much by way of punishment for the past, as of reformation for the future.

He divided the burden of government among a number of departments, as the council of war, the council of finance, the council of justice. This last was a court of supreme authority, both in civil and criminal matters, receiving appeals from the lower tribunals of the provinces, which were obliged to make a full report, every four months, or eighty days, of their own proceedings to this higher judicature. In all these bodies, a certain number of citizens were allowed to have seats with the nobles and professional dignitaries. There was, however, another body, a council of state, for aiding the king in the despatch of business, and advising him in matters of importance, which was drawn altogether from the highest order of chiefs. It consisted of fourteen members; and they had seats provided for them at the royal table.

Lastly, there was an extraordinary tribunal, called the council of music, but which, differing from the import of its name, was devoted to the encouragement of science and art. Works on astronomy, chronology, history, or any other science, were required to be submitted to its judgment, before they could be made public. This censorial power was of some moment, at least with regard to the historical department, where the wilful perversion of truth was made a capital offence by the bloody code of Nezahualcoyotl. Yet a Tezcucan author must have been a bungler, who could not elude a conviction under the cloudy veil of hieroglyphics. This body, which was drawn from the best instructed persons in the kingdom, with little regard to rank, had supervision of all the productions of art, and of the nicer fabrics. It decided on the qualifications of the professors in the various branches of science, on the fidelity of their instructions to their pupils, the deficiency of which was severely punished, and it instituted examinations of these latter. In short, it was a general board of education for the country. On stated days, historical compositions, and poems treating of moral or traditional topics, were recited before it by their authors. Seats were provided for the three crowned heads of the empire, who deliberated with the other members on the respective merits of the pieces, and distributed prizes of value to the successful competitors.

Such are the marvellous accounts transmitted to us of this institution; an institution certainly not to have been expected among the Aborigines of America. It is calculated to give us a higher idea of the refinement of the people, than even the noble architectural remains, which still cover some parts of the continent. Architecture is, to a certain extent, a sensual gratification. It addresses itself to the eye, and affords the best scope for the parade of barbaric pomp and splendor. It is the form in which the revenues of a semi-civilized people are most likely to be lavished. The most gaudy and ostentatious specimens of it, and sometimes the most stupendous, have been reared by such hands. It is one of the first steps in the great march of civilization. But the institution in question was evidence of still higher refinement. It was a literary luxury; and argued the existence of a taste in the nation, which relied for its gratification on pleasures of a purely intellectual character.

The influence of this academy must have been most propitious to the capital, which became the nursery, not only of such sciences as could be compassed by the scholarship of the period, but of various useful and ornamental arts. Its historians, orators, and poets were celebrated throughout the country. Its archives, for which accommodations were provided in the royal palace, were stored with the records of primitive ages. Its idiom, more polished than the Mexican, was, indeed, the purest of all the Nahuatlac dialects; and continued, long after the Conquest, to be that in which the best productions of the natives races were composed. Tezcuco claimed the glory of being the Athens of the Western World.

Among the most illustrious of her bards was the emperor himself,—for the Tezcucan writers claim this title for their chief, as head of the imperial alliance. He, doubtless, appeared as a competitor before that very academy where he so often sat as a critic. Many of his odes descended to a late generation, and are still preserved, perhaps, in some of the dusty repositories of Mexico or Spain. The historian, Ixtilxochitl, has left a translation, in Castilian, of one of the poems of his royal ancestor. It is not easy to render his version into corresponding English rhyme, without the perfume of the original escaping in this double filtration. They remind one of the rich breathings of Spanish-Arab poetry, in which an ardent imagination is tempered by a not unpleasing and moral melancholy. But, though sufficiently florid in diction, they are generally free from the meretricious ornaments and hyperbole with which the minstrelsy of the East is usually tainted. They turn on the vanities and mutability of human life; a topic very natural for a monarch who had himself experienced the strangest mutations of fortune. There is mingled in the lament of the Tezcucan bard, however, an Epicurean philosophy, which seeks relief from the fears of the future in the joys of the present. "Banish care", he says; "if there are bounds to pleasure, the saddest life must also have an end. Then weave the chaplet of flowers, and sing thy songs in praise of the all-powerful God;

for the glory of this world soon fadeth away. Rejoice in the green freshness of thy spring; for the day will come when thou shalt sigh for these joys in vain; when the sceptre shall pass from thy hands, thy servants shall wander desolate in thy courts, thy sons, and the sons of thy nobles, shall drink the dregs of distress, and all the pomp of thy victories and triumphs shall live only in their recollection. Yet the remembrance of the just shall not pass away from the nations, and the good thou hast done shall ever be held in honor. The goods of this life, its glories and its riches, are but lent to us, its substance is but an illusory shadow, and the things of to-day shall change on the coming of the morrow. Then gather the fairest flowers from thy gardens, to bind round thy brow, and seize the joys of the present, ere they perish".

But the hours of the Tezcucan monarch were not all passed in idle dalliance with the Muse, nor in the sober contemplations of philosophy, as at a later period. In the freshness of youth and early manhood he led the allied armies in their annual expeditions, which were certain to result in a wider extent of territory to the empire. In the intervals of peace he fostered those productive arts which are the surest sources of public prosperity. He encouraged agriculture above all; and there was scarcely a spot so rude, or a steep so inaccessible, as not to confess the power of cultivation. The land was covered with a busy population, and towns and cities sprung up in places since deserted, or dwindled into miserable villages.

From resources thus enlarged by conquest and domestic industry, the monarch drew the means for the large consumption of his own numerous household, and for the costly works which he executed for the convenience and embellishment of the capital. He filled it with stately edifices for his nobles, whose constant attendance he was anxious to secure at his court. He erected a magnificent pile of buildings which might serve both for a royal residence and for the public offices. It extended, from east to west, twelve hundred and thirty-four yards, and from north to south, nine hundred and seventy-eight. It was encompassed by a wall of unburnt bricks and cement, six feet wide and nine high, for one half of the circumference, and fifteen feet high for the other half. Within this inclosure were two courts. The outer one was used as the great market-place of the city; and continued to be so until long after the Conquest,— if, indeed, it is not now. The interior court was surrounded by the council-chambers and halls of justice. There were also accommodations there for the foreign ambassadors; and a spacious saloon, with apartments opening into it, for men of science and poets, who pursued their studies in this retreat, or met together to hold converse under its marble porticos. In this quarter, also, were kept the public archives; which fared better under the Indian dynasty, than they have since under their European successors.

Adjoining this court were the apartments of the king, including those for the royal harem, as liberally supplied with beauties as that of an Eastern sultan. Their walls were incrusted with alabasters, and richly tinted stucco, or hung with gorgeous tapestries of variegated feather-work. They led through long arcades, and through intricate labyrinths of shrubbery, into gardens, where baths and sparkling fountains were overshadowed by tall groves of cedar and cypress. The basins of water were well stocked with fish of various kinds, and the aviaries with birds glowing in all the gaudy plumage of the tropics. Many birds and animals, which could not be obtained alive, were represented in gold and silver so skilfully, as to have furnished the great naturalist, Hernandez, with models for his work.

Accommodations on a princely scale were provided for the sovereigns of Mexico and Tlacopan, when they visited the court. The whole of this lordly pile contained three hundred apartments, some of them fifty yards square. The height of the buildings is not mentioned. It was probably not great; but supplied the requisite room by the immense extent of ground which it covered. The interior was doubtless constructed of light materials, especially of the rich woods, which, in that country, are remarkable, when polished, for the brilliancy and variety of their colors. That the more solid materials of stone and stucco were also liberally employed is proved by the remains at the present day; remains, which have furnished an inexhaustible quarry for the churches and other edifices since erection by the Spaniards on the site of the ancient city.

We are not informed of the time occupied in building this palace. But two hundred thousand workmen, it is said, were employed on it! However this may be, it is certain that the Tezcucan monarchs, like those of Asia, and ancient Egypt, had the control of immense masses of men, and would sometimes turn the whole population of a conquered city, including the women, into the public works.—The most gigantic monuments of architecture which the world has witnessed would never have been reared by the hands of freemen.

Adjoining the palace were buildings for the king's children, who, by his various wives, amounted to no less than sixty sons and fifty daughters. Here they were instructed in all the exercises and accomplishments suited to their station; comprehending, what would scarcely find a place in a royal education on the other side of the Atlantic, the arts of working in metals, jewelry, and feather-mosaic. Once in every four months, the whole household, not excepting the youngest, and including all the officers and attendants on the king's person, assembled in a grand saloon of the

111

palace, to listen to a discourse from an orator, probably one of the priesthood. The princes, on this occasion, were all dressed in *nequen,* the coarsest manufacture of the country. The preacher began by enlarging on the obligations of morality, and of respect for the gods, especially important in persons whose rank gave such additional weight to example. He occasionally seasoned his homily with a pertinent application to his audience, if any member of it had been guilty of a notorious delinquency. From this wholesome admonition the monarch himself was not exempted, and the orator boldly reminded him of his paramount duty to show respect for his own laws. The king so far from taking umbrage, received the lesson with humility; and the audience, we are assured, were often melted into tears by the eloquence of the preacher. This curious scene may remind one of similar usages in the Asiatic and Egyptian despotisms, where the sovereign occasionally condescended to stoop from his pride of place, and allow his memory to be refreshed with the conviction of his own mortality. It soothed the feelings of the subject, to find himself thus placed, though but for a moment, on a level with his king; while it cost little to the latter, who was removed too far from his people, to suffer any thing by this short-lived familiarity. It is probable that such an act of public humiliation would have found less favor with a prince less absolute.

Nezahualcoyotl's fondness for magnificence was shown in his numerous villas, which were embellished with all that could make a rural retreat delightful. His favorite residence was at Tezcotzinco; a conical hill about two leagues from the capital. It was laid out in terraces, or hanging gardens, having a flight of steps five hundred and twenty in number, many of them hewn in the natural porphyry. In the garden on the summit was a reservoir of water, fed by an aqueduct that was carried over hill and valley, for several miles, on huge buttresses of masonry. A large rock stood in the midst of this basin, sculptured with the hieroglyphics representing the years of Nezahualcoyotl's reign and his principal achievements in each. On a lower level were three other reservoirs, in each of which stood a marble statue of a woman, emblematic of the three states of the empire. Another tank contained a winged lion, (?) cut out of the solid rock, bearing in his mouth the portrait of the emperor. His likeness had been executed in gold, wood, feather-work, and stone, but this was the only one which pleased him.

From these copious basins the water was distributed in numerous channels through the gardens, or was made to tumble over the rocks in cascades, shedding refreshing dews on the flowers and odoriferous shrubs below. In the depths of this fragrant wilderness, marble porticos and pavilions were erected, and baths excavated in the solid porphyry, which are still shown by the ignorant natives, as the "Baths of Montezuma"! The visitor descended by steps cut in the living stone, and polished so bright as to reflect like mirrors. Towards the base of the hill in the midst of cedar groves, whose gigantic branches threw a refreshing coolness over the verdure in the sultriest seasons of the year, rose the royal villa, with its light arcades and airy halls, drinking in the sweet perfumes of the gardens. Here the monarch often retired, to throw off the burden of state, and refresh his wearied spirits in the society of his favorite wives, reposing during the noontide heats in the embowering shades of his paradise, or mingling, in the cool of the evening, in their festive sports and dances. Here he entertained his imperial brothers of Mexico and Tlacopan, and followed the hardier pleasures of the chase in the noble woods that stretched for miles around his villa, flourishing in all their primeval majesty. Here, too, he often repaired in the latter days of his life, when age had tempered ambition and cooled the ardor of his blood, to pursue in solitude the studies of philosophy and gather wisdom from meditation.

The extraordinary accounts of the Tezcucan architecture are confirmed, in the main, by the relics which still cover the hill of Tezcotzinco, or are half buried beneath its surface. They attract little attention, indeed, in the country, where their true history has long since passed into oblivion; while the traveller, whose curiosity leads him to the spot, speculates on their probable origin, and, as he stumbles over the huge fragments of sculptured porphyry and granite, refers them to the primitive races who spread their colossal architecture over the country, long before the coming of the Acolhuans and the Aztecs.

Pipe-work at Tula

The Tezcucan princes were used to entertain a great number of concubines. They had but one lawful wife, to whose issue the crown descended. Nezahualcoyotl remained unmarried to a late period. He was disappointed in an early attachment, as the princess, who had been educated in privacy to be the partner of his throne, gave her hand to another. The injured monarch submitted the affair to the proper tribunal. The parties, however, were proved to have been ignorant of the destination of the lady, and the court, with an independence which reflects equal honor on the judges who could give, and the monarch who could receive the sentence, acquitted the young couple. This story is sadly contrasted by the following.

The king devoured his chagrin in the solitude of his beautiful villa of Tezcotzinco, or sought to divert it by travelling. On one of his journeys he was hospitably entertained by a potent vassal, the old lord of Tepechpan, who, to do his sovereign more honor, caused him to be attended at the banquet by a noble maiden, betrothed to himself, and who, after the fashion of the country, had been educated under his own roof. She was of the blood royal of Mexico, and nearly related, moreover, to the Tezcucan monarch. The latter, who had all the amorous temperament of the South, was captivated by the grace and personal charms of the youthful Hebe, and conceived a violent passion for her. He did not disclose it to any one, however, but, on his return home, resolved to gratify it, though at the expense of his own honor, by sweeping away the only obstacle which stood in his path.

He accordingly sent an order to the chief of Tepechpan to take command of an expedition set on foot against the Tlascalans. At the same time he instructed two Tezcucan chiefs to keep near the person of the old lord, and bring him into the thickest of the fight, where he might lose his life. He assured them, this

113

had been forfeited by a great crime, but that, from regard for his vassal's past services, he was willing to cover up his disgrace by an honorable death.

The veteran, who had long lived in retirement on his estates, saw himself, with astonishment, called so suddenly and needlessly into action, for which so many younger men were better fitted. He suspected the cause, and, in the farewell entertainment to his friends, uttered a presentiment of his sad destiny. His predictions were too soon verified and a few weeks placed the hand of his virgin bride at her own disposal.

Nezahualcoyotl did not think it prudent to break his passion publicly to the princess, so soon after the death of his victim. He opened a correspondence with her through a female relative, and expressed his deep sympathy for her loss. At the same time, he tendered the best consolation in his power, by an offer of his heart, and hand. Her former lover had been too well stricken in years for the maiden to remain long inconsolable. She was not aware of the perfidious plot against his life; and, after a decent time, she was ready to comply with her duty, by placing herself at the disposal of her royal kinsman.

It was arranged by the king, in order to give a more natural aspect to the affair, and prevent all suspicion of the unworthy part he had acted, that the princess should present herself in his grounds at Tezcotzinco, to witness some public ceremony there. Nezahualcoyotl was standing in a balcony of the palace, when she appeared, and inquired, as if struck with her beauty for the first time, "who the lovely young creature was, in his gardens". When his courtiers had acquainted him with her name and rank, he ordered her to be conducted to the palace, that she might receive the attentions due to her station. The interview was soon followed by a public declaration of his passion; and the marriage

was celebrated not long after, with great pomp, in the presence of his court, and of his brother monarchs of Mexico and Tlacopan.

This story, which furnishes so obvious a counterpart to that of David and Uriah, is told with great circumstantiality, both by the king's son and grandson, from whose narratives Ixtlilxochitl derived it. They stigmatize the action as the basest in their great ancestor's life. It is indeed too base not to leave an indelible stain on any character, however pure in other respects, and exalted.

The king was strict in the execution of his laws, though his natural disposition led him to temper justice with mercy. Many anecdotes are told of the benevolent interest he took in the concerns of his subjects, and of his anxiety to detect and reward merit, even in the most humble. It was common for him to ramble among them in disguise, like the celebrated caliph in the "Arabian Nights", mingling freely in conversation, and ascertaining their actual condition with his own eyes.

On one such occasion, when attended only by a single lord, he met with a boy who was gathering sticks in a field for fuel. He inquired of him "why he did not go into the neighbouring forest, where he would find a plenty of them". To which the lad answered, "It was the king's wood, and he would punish him with death, if he trespassed there". The royal forests were very extensive in Tezcuco, and were guarded by laws full as severe as those of the Norman tyrants in England. "What kind of man is your king?" asked the monarch, willing to learn the effect of these prohibitions on his own popularity. "A very hard man", answered the boy, "who denies his people what God has given them". Nezahualcoyotl urged him not to mind such arbitrary laws, but to glean his sticks in the forest, as there was no one present who would betray him. But the boy sturdily refused, bluntly accusing the disguised king, at the same time, of being a

114

traitor, and of wishing to bring him into trouble.

Nezahualcoyotl, on returning to the palace, ordered the child and his parents to be summoned before him. They received the orders with astonishment, but, on entering the presence, the boy at once recognised the person with whom he had discoursed so unceremoniously, and he was filled with consternation. The good-natured monarch, however, relieved his apprehensions, by thanking him for the lesson he had given him, and, at the same time, commended his respect for the laws, and praised his parents for the manner in which they had trained their son. He then dismissed the parties with a liberal largess; and afterwards mitigated the severity of the forest laws, so as to allow persons to gather any wood they might find on the ground, if they did not meddle with the standing timber.

Another adventure is told of him, with a poor woodman and his wife, who had brought their little load of billets for sale to the market-place of Tezcuco. The man was bitterly lamenting his hard lot, and the difficulty with which he earned a wretched subsistence, while the master of the palace before which they were standing lived an idle life, without toil, and with all the luxuries in the world at his command.

He was going on in his complaints, when the good woman stopped him, by reminding him he might be overheard. He was so, by Nezahualcoyotl himself, who, standing, screened from observation, at a latticed window, which overlooked the market, was amusing himself, as he was wont, with observing the common people chaffering in the square. He immediately ordered the querulous couple into his presence. They appeared trembling and conscience-struck before him. The king gravely inquired what they had said. As they answered him truly, he told

them they should reflect, that, if he had great treasures at his command, he had still greater calls for them; that, far from leading an easy life, he was oppressed with the whole burden of government; and concluded by admonishing them "to be more cautious in future, as walls had ears". He then ordered his officers to bring a quantity of cloth, and a generous supply of cacao, (the coin of the country), and dismissed them. "Go", said he; "with the little you now have, you will be rich; while, with all my riches, I shall still be poor".

It was not his passion to hoard. He dispensed his revenues munificently, seeking out poor, but meritorious objects, on whom to bestow them. He was particularly mindful of disabled soldiers, and those who had in any way sustained loss in the public service; and, in case of their death, extended assistance to their surviving families. Open mendicity was a thing he would never tolerate, but chastised it with exemplary rigor.

It would be incredible, that a man of the enlarged mind and endowments of Nezahualcoyotl should acquiesce in the sordid superstitions of his countrymen, and still more in the sanguinary rites borrowed by them from the Aztecs. In truth, his humane temper shrunk from these cruel ceremonies, and he strenuously endeavoured to recall his people to the more pure and simple worship of the ancient Toltecs. A circumstance produced a temporary change in his conduct.

He had been married some years to the wife he had so unrighteously obtained, but was not blessed with issue. The priests represented that it was owing to his neglect of the gods of his country, and that his only remedy was, to propitiate them by human sacrifice. The king reluctantly consented, and the altars once more smoked with the blood of slaughtered captives. But it was all in vain; and he indignantly exclaimed, "These idols of wood and stone can neither hear nor feel; much less could they make the heavens, and the earth, and man, the lord of it. These must be the work of the all-powerful, unknown God, Creator of the universe, on whom alone I must rely for consolation and support".

He then withdrew to his rural palace of Tezcotzinco, where he remained forty days, fasting and praying at stated hours, and offering up no other sacrifice, than the sweet incense of copal, and aromatic herbs and gums. At the expiration of this time, he is said to have been comforted by a vision assuring him of the success of his petition. At all events, such proved to be the fact; and this was followed by the cheering intelligence of the triumph of his arms in a quarter where he had lately experienced some humiliating reverses.

Greatly strengthened in his former religious convictions, he now openly professed his faith, and was more earnest to wean his subjects from their degrading superstitions, and to substitute nobler and more spiritual conceptions of the Deity. He built a temple in the usual pyramidal form, and on the summit a tower nine stories high, to represent the nine heavens; a tenth was surmounted by a roof painted black, and profusely gilded with stars, on the outside, and incrusted with metals and precious stones within. He dedicated this to *the unknown God, the Cause of causes*. It seems probable, from the emblem on the tower, as well as from the complexion of his verses, as we shall see, that he mingled with the reverence for the Supreme the astral worship which existed among the Toltecs. Various musical instruments were placed on the top among the Toltecs. Various musical instruments were placed on the top of the tower, and the sound of them, accompanied by the ringing of a sonorous metal struck by a mallet, summoned the worshippers to prayers, at regular seasons. No image was allowed in the edifice, as unsuited to the "invisible God"; and the people were expressly prohibited from profaning the altars with blood, or any other sacrifices than that of the perfume of flowers and sweet-scented gums.

The remainder of his days was chiefly spent in his delicious solitudes of Tezcotzinco, where he devoted himself to astronomical and, probably, astrological studies, and to meditation on his immortal destiny,—giving utterance to his feelings in songs, or rather hymns, of much solemnity and pathos. An extract from one of these will convey some idea of his religious speculations. The pensive tenderness of the verses quoted in a preceding page is deepened here into a mournful, and even gloomy coloring; while the wounded spirit, instead of seeking relief in the convivial sallies of a young and buoyant temperament, turns for consolation to the world beyond the grave.

"All things on earth have their term, and, in the most joyous career of their vanity and splendor, their strength fails, and they sink into the dust. All the round world is but a sepulchre; and there is nothing, which lives on its surface, that shall not be hidden and entombed beneath it. Rivers, torrents, and streams move onward to their destination. Not one flows back to its pleasant source. They rush onward, hastening to bury themselves in the deep bosom of the ocean. The things of yesterday are no more to-day; and the things of to-day shall cease, perhaps, on the morrow. The cemetery is full of the loathsome dust of bodies once quickened by living souls, who occupied thrones, presided over assemblies, marshalled armies, subdued

Education scenes, from a Codex.

116

provinces, arrogated to themselves worship, were puffed up with vainglorious pomp, and power, and empire.

"But these glories have all passed away, like the fearful smoke that issues from the throat of Popocatepetl, with no other memorial of their existence than the record on the page of the chronicler.

"The great, the wise, the valiant, the beautiful—alas! where are they now? They are all mingled with the clod; and that which has befallen them shall happen to us, and to those that come after us. Yet let us take courage, illustrious nobles and chieftains, true friends and loyal subjects,—*let us aspire to that heaven, where all is eternal, and corruption cannot come.* The horrors of the tomb are but the cradle of the Sun, and the dark shadows of death are brilliant lights for the stars". The mystic import of the last sentence seems to point to that superstition respecting the mansions of the Sun, which forms so beautiful a contrast to the dark features of the Aztec mythology.

At length, about the year 1470, Nezahualcoyotl, full of years and honors, felt himself drawing near his end. Almost half a century had elapsed since he mounted the throne of Tezcuco. He had found the kingdom dismenbered by faction, and bowed to the dust beneath the yoke of a foreign tyrant. He had broken that yoke; had breathed new life into the nation, renewed its ancient institutions, extended wide its domain; had seen it flourishing in all the activity of trade and agriculture, gathering strength from its enlarged resources, and daily advancing higher and higher in the great march of civilization. All this he had seen, and might fairly attribute no small portion of it to his own wise and beneficent rule. His long and glorious day was now drawing to its close; and he contemplated the event with the same serenity, which he had shown under the clouds of its morning and in its meridian splendor.

A short time before his death, he gathered around him those of his children in whom he most confided, his chief counsellors, the ambassadors of Mexico, and Tlacopan, and his little son, the heir to the crown, his only offspring by the queen. He was then not eight years old; but had already given, as far as so tender a blossom might, the riche promise of future excellence.

After tenderly embracing the child, the dying monarch threw over him the robes of sovereignty. He then gave audience to the ambassadors, and, when they had retired, made the boy repeat the substance of the conversation. He followed this by such counsels as were suited to his comprehension, and which, when remembered through the long vista of after years, would serve as lights to guide him in his government of the kingdom. He besought him not to neglect the worship of "the unknown God", regretting that he himself had been unworthy to know him, and intimating his conviction that the time would come when he should be known and worshipped throughout the land.

He next addressed himself to that one of his sons, in whom he placed the greatest trust, and whom he had selected as the guardian of the realm. "From this hour", said he to him, "you will fill the place that I have filled, of father to this child; you will teach him to live as he ought; and by your counsels he will rule over the empire. Stand in his place, and be his guide, till he shall be of age to govern for

Right: sitting figure: pre-Aztec art.

118

Left: the goddess of the Earth; right: a statuette called Atlantes. These two very old statuettes can be seen at the National Museum of Anthropology of Mexico.

Left: this very old figure of a sitting priest (about 12 inches high) has been called "the Scribe". Right: figure with a rich head-dress and feather ornaments-a nobleman. "The allegorical phantasms of his religion, no doubt, gave a direction to the Aztec artist, in the delineation of the human figure... As these superstitions lost their hold on his mind, it opened to the influence of a purer taste".

himself". Then, turning to his other children, he admonished them to live united with one another, and to show all loyalty to their prince, who though a child, already manifested a discretion far above his years. "Be true to him", he added, "and he will maintain you in your rights and dignities".

Feeling his end approaching, he exclaimed, "Do not bewail me with idle lamentations. But sing the song of gladness, and show a courageous spirit, that the nations I have subdued may not believe you disheartened, but may feel that each one of you is strong enough to keep them in obedience!" The undaunted spirit of the monarch shone forth even in the agonies of death. That stout heart, however, melted, as he took leave of his children and friends, weeping tenderly over them, while he bade each a last adieu. When they had withdrawn, he ordered the officers of the palace to allow no one to enter it again. Soon after, he expired, in the seventy-second year of his age, and the forty-third of his reign.

Thus died the greatest monarch, and, if one foul blot could be effaced, perhaps the best, who ever sat upon an Indian throne. His character is delineated with tolerable impartiality by his kinsman, the Tezcucan chronicler. "He was wise, valiant, liberal; and, when we consider the magnanimity of his soul, the grandeur and success of his enterprises, his deep policy, as well as daring, we must admit him to have far surpassed every other prince and captain of this New World. He had few failings himself, and rigorously punished those of others. He preferred the public to his private interest; was most charitable in his nature, often buying articles, at double their worth, of poor and honest persons, and giving them away again to the sick and infirm. In seasons of scarcity he was particularly bountiful, remitting the taxes of his vassals, and supplying their wants from the royal granaries. He put no faith in the idolatrous worship of the country. He was well instructed in moral science, and sought, above all things, to obtain light for knowing the true God. He believed in one God only, the Creator of heaven and earth, by whom we have our being, who never revealed himself to us in human form, nor in any ofter; with whom the souls of the virtuous are to dwell after death, while the wicked will suffer pains unspeakable. He invoked the Most High, as "He by whom we live", and "Who has all things in himself". He recognised the Sun for his father, and the Earth for his mother. He taught his children not to confide in idols, and only to conform to the outward worship of them with deference to public opinion. If he could not entirely abolish human sacrifices, derived from the Aztecs, he, at least, restricted them to slaves and captives".

I have occupied so much space with this illustrious prince, that but little remains for his son and successor, Nezahualpilli. I have thougt it better, in our narrow limits, to present a complete view of a single epoch, the most interesting in the Tezcucan annals, than to spread the inquiries over a broader, but comparatively barren field. Yet Nezahualpilli, the heir to the crown, was a remarkable person, and his reign contains many incidents, which I regret to be obliged to pass over in silence.

He had, in many respects, a taste similar to his father's, and, like him, displayed a profuse magnificence in his way of living and in his public edifices. He was more severe in his morals; and, in the execution of justice, stern even to the sacrifice of natural affection. Several remarkable instances of this are told; one, among others, in relation to his eldest son, the heir to the crown, a prince of great promise. The young man entered into a poetical correspondence with one of his father's concubines, the lady of Tula, as she was called, a woman of humble origin, but of uncommon endowments. She wrote verses with ease, and could discuss graver matters with the king and his ministers. She maintained a separate establishment, where she lived in state, and acquired, by her beauty and accomplishments, great ascendency over her royal lover. With this favorite the prince carried on a correspondence in verse,—whether of an amorous nature does not appear. At all events, the offence was capital. It was submitted to the regular tribunal, who pronounced sentence of death on the unfortunate youth; and the king, steeling his heart against all entreaties and the voice of nature, suffered the cruel judgment to be carried into execution. We might, in this case, suspect the influence of baser passions on his mind, but it was not a solitary instance of his inexorable justice towards those most near to him. He had the stern virtue of an ancient Roman, destitute of the softer graces which make virtue attractive. When the sentence was carried into effect, he shut himself up in his palace for many weeks, and commanded the doors and windows of his son's residence to be walled up, that it might never again be occupied.

Nezahualpilli resembled his father in his passion for astronomical studies, and is said to have had an observatory on one of his palaces. He was devoted to war in his youth, but, as he advanced in years, resigned himself to a more indolent way of life, and sought his chief amusement in the pursuit of his favorite science, or in the soft pleasures of the sequestered gardens of Tezcotzinco. This quiet life was ill suited to the turbulent temper of the times, and of his Mexican rival, Montezuma. The distant provinces fell off from their allegiance; the army relaxed its discipline; disaffection crept into its ranks; and the wily Montezuma, partly by violence, and partly by stratagems unworthy of a king, succeeded in plundering his brother monarch of some of his most valuable domains. Then

it was, that he arrogated to himself the title and supremacy of emperor, hitherto borne by the Tezcucan princes, as head of the alliance. Such is the account given by the historians of that nation, who, in this way, explain the acknowledged superiority of the Aztec sovereign, both in territory and consideration, on the landing of the Spaniards.

These misfortunes pressed heavily on the spirits of Nezahualpilli. Their effect was increased by certain gloomy prognostics of a near calamity which was to overwhelm the country. He withdrew to his retreat, to brood in secret over his sorrows. His health rapidly declined; and in the year 1515, at the age of fifty-two, he sunk into the grave, happy, at least, that, by this timely death, he escaped witnessing the fulfilment of his own predictions, in the ruin of his country, and the extinction of the Indian dynasties, for ever.

In reviewing the brief sketch here presented of the Tezcucan monarchy, we are strongly impressed with the conviction of its superiority, in all the great features of civilization, over the rest of Anahuac. The Mexicans showed a similar proficiency, no doubt, in the mechanic arts, and even in mathematical science. But in the science of government, in legislation, in speculative doctrines of a religious nature, in the more elegant pursuits of poetry, eloquence, and whatever depended on refinement of taste and a polished idiom, they confessed themselves inferior, by resorting to their rivals for instruction, and citing their works as the masterpieces of their tongue. The best histories, the best poems, the best code of laws, the purest dialect, were all allowed to be Tezcucan. The Aztecs rivalled their neighbours in splendor of living, and even in the magnificence of their structures. They displayed a pomp and ostentatious pageantry, truly Asiatic. But this was the development of the material, rather than the intellectual principle. They wanted the refinement of manners essential to a continued advance in civilization. An insurmountable limit was put to theirs, by that bloody mythology, which threw its withering taint over the very air that they breathed.

The superiority of the Tezcucans was owing, doubtless, in a great measure, to that of the two sovereigns whose reigns we have been depicting. There is no position, which affords such scope for ameliorating the condition of man, as that occupied by an absolute ruler over a nation imperfectly civilized. From his elevated place, commanding all the resources of his age, it is in his power to diffuse them far and wide among his people. He may be the copious reservoir on the mountain top, drinking in the dews of heaven, to send them in fertilizing streams along the lower slopes and valleys, clothing even the wilderness in beauty. Such were Nezahual-coyotl, and his illustrious successor, whose enlightened policy, extending through nearly a century, wrought a most salutary revolution in the condition of their country. It is remarkable that we, the inhabitants of the same continent, should be more familiar with the history of many a barbarian chief, both in the Old and New World, than with that of these truly great men, whose names are identified with the most glorious period in the annals of the Indian races.

What was the actual amount of the Tezcucan civilization, it is not easy to determine, with the imperfect light afforded us. It was certainly far below any thing, which the word conveys, measured by a European standard. In some of the arts, and in any walk of science, they could only have made, as it were, a beginning. But they had begun in the right way, and already showed a refinement in sentiment and manners, a capacity for receiving instruction, which, under good auspices, might have led them on to indefinite improvement. Unhappily, they were fast falling under the dominion of the warlike Aztecs. And that people repaid the benefits received from their more polished neighbors by imparting to them their own ferocious superstition, which, falling like a mildew on the land, would soon have blighted its rich blossoms of promise, and turned even its fruits to dust and ashes.

Below: remains of a temple, at Mitla. Right: there is in these figures of Tula something as mysterious as in the Sphinx of Ancient Egypt...

Origin of the Mexican Civilization - Analogies with the Old World.

Left: a kind of mosaic of sculptured stones at Mitla.
Below: This very expressive head can be seen at the Museum of Mexico.

When the Europeans first touched the shores of America, it was as if they had alighted on another planet,—every thing there was so different from what they had before seen. They were introduced to new varieties of plants, and to unknown races of animals; while man, the lord of all, was equally strange, in complexion, language, and institutions. It was what they emphatically styled it, a New World. Taught by their faith to derive all created beings from one source, they felt a natural perplexity as to the manner in which these distant and insulated regions could have obtained their inhabitants. The same curiosity was felt by their countrymen at home, and the European scholars bewildered their brains with speculations on the best way of solving this interesting problem.

In accounting for the presence of animals there, some imagined that the two hemispheres might once have been joined in the extreme North, so as to have afforded an easy communication. Others, embarrassed by the difficulty of transporting inhabitants of the tropics across the Arctic regions, revived the old story of Plato's Atlantis, that huge island, now submerged, which might have stretched from the shores of Africa to the eastern borders of the new continent; while they saw vestiges of a similar convulsion of nature in the green islands sprinkled over the Pacific, once the mountain summits of a vast continent, now buried beneath the waters. Some, distrusting the existence of revolutions, of which no record was preserved, supposed that animals might have found their way across the ocean by various means; the birds of stronger wing by flight over the narrowest spaces; while the tamer kinds of quadrupeds might easily have been transported by men in boats, and even the most ferocious, as tigers, bears, and the like, have been brought over in the same manner, when young, "for amusement and the pleasure of the chase!". Others, again, maintained the equally probable opinion, that angels, who had, doubtless, taken charge of them in the ark, had also superintended their distribution afterwards over the different parts of the globe. Such were the extremities to which even thinking minds were reduced, in their eagerness to reconcile the literal interpretation of Scripture with the phenomena of nature! The philosophy of a later day conceives that it is no departure from this sacred authority to follow the suggestions of science, by referring the new tribes of animals to a creation, since the deluge, in those places for which they were clearly intended by constitution and habits.

Man would not seem to present the same embarrassments, in the discussion, as the inferior orders. He is fitted by nature for every climate, the burning sun of the tropics and the icy atmosphere of the North. He wanders indifferently over the sands of the desert, the waste of polar snows, and the pathless ocean. Neither mountains nor seas intimidate him, and, by the aid of mechanical contrivances, he accomplishes journeys which birds of boldest wing would perish in attempting. Without ascending to the high northern latitudes, where the continents of Asia and America approach within fifty miles of each other, it would be easy for the inhabitant of Eastern Tartary or Japan to steer his canoe from islet to islet, quite across to the American shore, without ever being on the ocean more than two days at a time. The communication is somewhat more difficult on the Atlantic side. But even there, Iceland was occupied by colonies of Europeans many hundred years before the discovery by Columbus; and the transit from Iceland to America is comparatively easy. Independently of these channels, others were opened in the southern hemisphere, by means of the numerous islands in the Pacific. The population of America is not nearly so difficult

a problem, as that of these little spots. But experience shows how practicable the communication may have been, even with such sequestered places. The savage has been picked up in his canoe, after drifting hundreds of leagues on the open ocean, and sustaining life, for months, by the rain from heaven, and such fish as he could catch. The instances are not very rare; and it would be strange, if these wandering barks should not sometimes have been intercepted by the great continent, which stretches across the globe, in unbroken continuity, almost from pole to pole. No doubt, history could reveal to us more than one example of men, who, thus driven upon the American shores, have mingled their blood with that of the primitive races who occupied them.

The real difficulty is not, as with the animals, to explain how man could have reached America, but from what quarter he actually has reached it. In surveying the whole extent of the New World, it was found to contain two great families, one in the lowest stage of civilization, composed of hunters, and another nearly as far advanced in refinement as the semi-civilized empires of Asia. The more polished races were probably unacquainted with the existence of each other, on the different continents of America, and had as little intercourse with the barbarian tribes, by whom they were surrounded. Yet they had some things in common both with these last and with one another, which remarkably distinguished them from the inhabitants of the Old World. They had a common complexion and physical organization,—at least, bearing a more uniform character than is found among the nations of any other quarter of the globe. They had some usages and institutions in common, and spoke languages of similar construction, curiously distinguished from those on the eastern hemisphere.

Whence did the refinement of these more polished races come? Was it only a higher development of the same Indian character, which we see, in the more northern latitudes, defying every attempt at permanent civilization? Was it engrafted on a race of higher order in the scale originally, but self-instructed, working its way upward by its own powers? Was it, in short, an indigenous civilization? or was it borrowed in some degree from the nations in the Eastern World? If indigenous, how are we to explain the singular coincidence with the East in institutions and opinions? If Oriental, how shall we account for the great dissimilarity in language, and for the ignorance of some of the most simple and useful arts,

which, once known, it would seem scarcely possible should have been forgotten? This is the riddle of the Sphinx, which no Œdipus has yet had the ingenuity to solve. It is, however, a question of deep interest to every curious and intelligent observer of his species. And it has accordingly occupied the thoughts of men, from the first discovery of the country to the present time; when the extraordinary monuments brought to light in Central America have given a new impulse to inquiry, by suggesting the probability,—the possibility, rather,—that surer evidences than any hitherto known might be afforded for establishing the fact of a positive communication with the other hemisphere.

It is not my intention to add many pages to the volumes already written on this inexhaustible topic. The subject—as remarked by a writer, of a philosophical mind himself, and who has done more than any other for the solution of the mystery—is of too speculative a nature for history, almost a philosophy. But this work would be incomplete, without affording the reader the means of judging for himself as to the true sources of the peculiar civilization already described, by exhibiting to him the alleged points of resemblance with the ancient continent. In doing this, I shall confine myself to my proper subject, the Mexicans, or to what, in some way or other, may have a bearing on this subject; proposing to state only real points of resemblance, as they are supported by evidence, and stripped, as far as possible, of the illusions with which they have been invested by the pious credulity of one party, and the visionary system-building of another.

An obvious analogy is found in *cosmogonal traditions,* and *religious usages.* The reader has already been made acquainted with the Aztec system of four great cycles, at the end of each of which the world was destroyed, to be again regenerated. The belief in these periodical convulsions of nature, through the agency of some one or other of the elements, was familiar to many countries in the eastern hemisphere; and, though varying in detail, the general resemblance of outline furnishes an argument in favor of a common origin.

No tradition has been more widely spread among nations than that of a Deluge. Independently of tradition, indeed, it would seem to be naturally suggested by the interior structure of the earth, and by the elevated places on which marine substances are found to be deposited. It was the received notion, under some form or other, of the most civilized people in the Old World, and of the barbarians of the New. The Aztecs combined with this some particular circumstances of a more arbitrary character, resembling the accounts of the East. They believed that two persons survived the deluge, a man, named Coxcox, and his wife. Their heads are represented in ancient paintings, together with a boat floating on the waters, at the foot of a mountain. A dove is also depicted, with the hieroglyphical emblem of languages in his mouth, which he is distributing to the children of Coxcox, who were born dumb. The neighboring people of Michuacan, inhabiting the same high plains of the Andes, had a still further tradition, that the boat, in which Tezpi, their Noah, escaped, was filled with various kinds of animals and birds. After some time, a vulture was sent out from it, but remained feeding on the dead bodies of the giants, which had been left on the earth, as the waters subsided. The little humming-bird, *huitzitzilin,* was sent forth, and returned with a twig in its mouth. The coincidence of both these accounts with the Hebrew and Chaldean narratives is obvious. It were to be wished that the authority for the Michuacan version were more satisfactory.

On the way between Vera Cruz and the

capital, not far from the modern city of Puebla, stands the venerable relic,—with which the reader has become familiar in the course of the narrative,—called the temple of Cholula. It is, as he will remember, a pyramidal mound, built, or rather cased, with unburnt brick, rising to the height of nearly one hundred and eighty feet. The popular tradition of the natives is, that it was erected by a family of giants, who had escaped the great inundation, and designed to raise the building to the clouds; but the gods, offended with their presumption, sent fires from heaven on the pyramid, and compelled them to abandon the attempt. The partial coincidence of this legend with the Hebrew account of the tower of Babel, received, also, by other nations of the East, cannot be denied. But one, who has not examined the subject, will scarcely credit what bold hypotheses have been reared on this slender basis.

Another point of coincidence is found in the goddess Cioacoatl, "our lady and mother"; "the first goddess who brought forth"; "who bequeathed the sufferings of childbirth to women, as the tribute of death"; "by whom sin came into the world". Such was the remarkable language applied by the Aztecs to this venerated deity. She was usually represented with a serpent near her; and her name signified the "serpent-woman". In all this we see much to remind us of the mother of the human family, the Eve of the Hebrew nations.

But none of the deities of the country suggested such astonishing analogies with Scripture, as Quetzalcoatl, with whom the reader has already been made acquainted. He was the white man, wearing a long beard, who came from the East; and who, after presiding over the golden age of Anahuac, disappeared as mysteriously as he had come, on the great Atlantic Ocean. As he promised to return at some future day, his reappearance was looked for with confidence by each succeeding generation. There is little in these circumstances to remind one of Christianity. But the curious antiquaries of Mexico found out, that to this god were to be referred the institution of ecclesiastical communities, reminding one of the monastic societies of the Old World; that of the rites of confession and penance; and the knowledge even of the great doctrines of the Trinity and the Incarnation! One party, with pious industry, accumulated proofs to establish his identity with the Apostle St. Thomas; while another, with less scrupulous faith, saw, in his anticipated advent to regenerate the nation, the type, dim-veiled,

The reign of Montezuma, the last emperor of the Aztecs, from a Codex.

of the Messiah!

Yet we should have charity for the missionaries who first landed in this world of wonders; where, while man and nature wore so strange an aspect, they were astonished by occasional glimpses of rites and ceremonies, which reminded them of a purer faith. In their amazement, they did not reflect, whether these things were not the natural expression of the religious feeling common to all nations who have reached even a moderate civilization. They did not inquire, whether the same things were not practised by other idolatrous people. They could not suppress their wonder, as they beheld the Cross, the sacred emblem of their own faith, raised as an object of worship in the temples of Anahuac. They met with it in various places; and the image of a cross may be seen at this day, sculptured in bas-relief, on the walls of one of the buildings of Palenque, while a figure bearing some resemblance to that of a child is held up to it, as if in adoration.

Their surprise was heightened, when they witnessed a religious rite which reminded them of the Christian communion. On these occasions an image of the tutelary deity of the Aztecs was made of the flour of maize, mixed with blood, and, after consecration by the priests, was distributed among the people, who, as they ate it, "showed signs of humiliation and sorrow, declaring it was the flesh of the deity!" How could the Roman Catholic fail to recognise the awful ceremony of the Eucharist?

With the same feelings they witnessed another ceremony, that of the Aztec baptism; in which, after a solemn invocation, the head and lips of the infant were touched with water, and a name was given to it; while the goddess Cioacoatl, who presided over childbirth, was implored, "that the sin, which was given to us before the beginning of the world, might not visit the child, but that, cleansed by these waters, it might live and be born anew!"

It is true, these several rites were attended with many peculiarities, very unlike those in any Christian church. But the fathers fastened their eyes exclusively on the points of resemblance. They were not aware, that the Cross was the symbol of worship, of the highest antiquity, in Egypt and Syria; and that rites, resembling those of communion and baptism, were practised by Pagan nations, on whom the light of Christianity had never shone. In their amazement, they not only magnified what they saw, but were perpetually cheated by the illusions of their own heated imaginations. In this they were admirably assisted by their Mexican converts, proud to establish—and half believing it themselves—a correspondence between their own faith, and that of their conquerors.

The ingenuity of the chronicler was taxed to find out analogies between the Aztec and Scripture histories, both old and new. The migration from Aztlan to Anahuac was typical of the Jewish exodus. The places, where the Mexicans halted on the march, were identified with those in the journey of the Israelites; and the name of Mexico itself was found to be nearly identical with the Hebrew name for the Messiah. The Mexican hieroglyphics afforded a boundless field for the display of this critical acuteness. The most remarkable passages in the Old and New Testaments were read in their mysterious characters; and the eye of faith could trace there the whole story of the Passion, the Saviour suspended from the cross, and the Virgin Mary with her attendant angels!

The Jewish and Christian schemes were strangely mingled together, and the brains of the good fathers were still further bewildered by the mixture of heathenish abominations, which were so closely intertwined with the most orthodox observances. In their per-plexity, they looked on the whole as the delusion of the Devil, who counterfeited the rites of Christianity and the traditions of the chosen people, that he might allure his wretched victims to their own destruction.

But, although it is not necessary to resort to this startling supposition, nor even to call up an apostle from the dead, or any later missionary, to explain the coincidences with Christianity; yet these coincidences must be allowed to furnish an argument in favor of some primitive communication with that great brotherhood of nations on the old continent, among whom similar ideas have been so widely diffused. The probability of such a communication, especially with Eastern Asia, is much strengthened by the resemblance of sacerdotal institutions, and of some religious rites, as those of marriage, and the burial of the dead; by the practice of human sacrifices, and even of cannibalism, traces of which are discernible in the Mongol races; and, lastly, by a conformity of social usages and manners, so striking that the description of Montezuma's court may well pass for that of the Grand Khan's, as depicted by Maundeville and Marco Polo. It would occupy too much room to go into details in this matter, without which, however, the strength of the argument

These stelae at Monte Alban, in the "second temple of dancing" present men practising this art (left and right).

Left and right: other "dancers" at Monte Alban.—"They danced gracefully, to the sound of various instruments, accompanying their movements with chants, of a pleasing, though somewhat plaintive character".

cannot be felt, nor fully established. It has been done by others; and an occasional coincidence has been adverted to in the preceding chapter.

It is true, we should be very slow to infer identity, or even correspondence, between nations, from a partial resemblance of habits and institutions. Where this relates to manners, and is founded on caprice, it is not more conclusive than when it flows from the spontaneous suggestions of nature, common to all. The resemblance, in the one case, may be referred to accident; in the other, to the constitution of man. But there are certain arbitrary peculiarities, which, when found in different nations, reasonably suggest the idea of some previous communication between them. Who can doubt the existence of an affinity, or, at least, intercourse, between tribes, who had the same strange habit of burying the dead in a sitting posture, as was practised, to some extent, by most, if not all, of the Aborigines, from Canada to Patagonia? The habit of burning the dead, familiar to both Mongols and Aztecs, is, in itself, but slender proof of a common origin. The body must be disposed of in some way; and this, perhaps, is as natural as any other. But, when to this is added the circumstance of collecting the ashes in a vase, and depositing the single article of a precious stone along with them, the coincidence is remarkable. Such minute coincidences are not unfrequent; while the accumulation of those of a more general character, though individually of little account, greatly strengthens the probability of a communication with the East.

A proof of a higher kind is found in the analogies of *science.* We have seen the peculiar chronological system of the Aztecs; their method of distributing the years into cycles, and of reckoning by means of periodical series, instead of numbers. A similar process was used by the various Asiatic nations of the Mongol family, from India to Japan. Their cycles, indeed, consisted of sixty, instead of fifty-two years; and for the terms of their periodical series, they employed the names of the elements, and the signs of the zodiac, of which latter the Mexicans, probably, had no knowledge. But the principle was precisely the same.

A correspondence quite as extraordinary is found between the hieroglyphics used by the Aztecs for the signs of the days, and those zodiacal signs which the Eastern Asiatics employed as one of the terms of their series. The symbols in the Mongolian calendar are borrowed from animals. Four of the twelve are the same as the Aztec. Three others are as nearly the same as the different species of animals in the two hemispheres would allow. The remaining five refer to no creature then found in Anahuac. The resemblance went as far as it could. The similarity of these conventional symbols, among the several nations of the East, can hardly fail to carry conviction of a common origin for the system, as regards them. Why should not a similar conclusion be applied to the Aztec calendar, which, although relating to days, instead of years, was, like the Asiatic, equally appropriated to chronological uses, and to those of divination?

I shall pass over the further resemblance to the Persians, shown in the adjustment of time by a similar system of intercalation; and to the Egyptians, in the celebration of the remarkable festival of the winter solstice; since, although sufficiently curious, the coincidences might be accidental, and add little to the weight of evidence offered by an agreement in combinations, of so complex and artificial a character, as those before stated.

Amidst these intellectual analogies, one would expect to meet with that of *language,* the vehicle of intellectual communication, which usually exhibits traces of its origin, even when the science and literature, that are embodied in it, have widely diverged. No inquiry, however, has led to less satisfactory results. The languages spread over the western continent far exceed in number those found in any equal population in the eastern. They exhibit the remarkable anomaly of differing as widely in etymology as they agree in organization; and, on the other hand, while they bear some slight affinity to the languages of the Old World in the former particular, they have no resemblance to them whatever in the latter. The Mexican was spoken for an extent of three hundred leagues. But within the boundaries of New Spain more than twenty languages were found; not simply dialects, but, in many instances, radically different. All these idioms, however, with one exception, conformed to that peculiar synthetic structure, by which every Indian dialect appears to have been fashioned, from the land of the Esquimaux to Terra del Fuego; a system, which, bringing the greatest number of ideas within the smallest possible compass, condenses whole sentences into a single word, displaying a curious mechanism, in which some discern the hand of the philosopher, and others only the spontaneous efforts of the savage.

The etymological affinities detected with the ancient continent are not very numerous, and they are drawn indiscriminately from all the tribes scattered over America. On the whole, more analogies have been found with the idioms of Asia, than of any other quarter. But their amount is too inconsiderable to balance the opposite conclusion inferred by a total dissimilarity of structure. A remarkable exception is found in the Othomi or Otomie language, which covers a wider territory than any other but the Mexican, in New Spain; and which, both in its monosyllabic composition, so different from those around it, and in its vocabulary, shows a very singular affinity to the Chinese. The existence of this insulated idiom, in the heart of this vast continent, offers a curious theme for speculation, entirely beyond the province of history.

The American languages, so numerous and widely diversified, present an immense field of inquiry, which, notwithstanding the labors of several distinguished philologists, remains yet to be explored. It is only after a wide comparison of examples, that conclusions founded on analogy can be trusted. The difficulty of making such comparisons increases with time, from the facility which the peculiar structure of the Indian languages affords for new combinations; while the insensible influence of contact with civilized man, in producing these, must lead to a still further distrust of our conclusions.

The theory of an Asiatic origin for Aztec civilization derives stronger confirmation from the light of *tradition,* which, shining steadily from the far North-west, pierces through the dark shadows that history and mythology have alike thrown around the antiquities of the country. Traditions of a Western, or North-western origin were found among the more barbarous tribes, and by the Mexicans were preserved both orally and in their hieroglyphical maps, where the different stages of their migration are carefully noted. But who, at this day, shall read them? They are admitted to agree, however, in representing the populous North as the prolific hive of the American races. In this quarter were placed their Aztlan, and their Huehueta-pallan; the bright abodes of their ancestors, whose warlike exploits rivalled those which the Teutonic nations have recorded of Odin and the mythic heroes of Scandinavia. From this quarter the Toltecs, the Chichemecs, and the kindred races of the Nahuatlacs, came

144

successively up the great plateau of the Andes, spreading over its hills and valleys, down to the Gulf of Mexico.

Antiquaries have industriously sought to detect some still surviving traces of these migrations. In the north-western districts of New Spain, at a thousand miles' distance from the capital, dialects have been discovered, showing intimate affinity with the Mexican. Along the Rio Gila, remains of populous towns are to be seen, quite worthy of the Aztecs in their style of architecture. The country north of the great Rio Colorado has been imperfectly explored; but, in the higher latitudes, in the neighborhood of Nootka, tribes still exist, whose dialects, both in the termination and general sound of the words, bear considerable resemblance to the Mexican. Such are the vestiges, few, indeed, and feeble, that still exist to attest the truth of traditions, which themselves have remained steady and consistent, through the lapse of centuries, and the migrations of races.

The conclusions suggested by the intellectual and moral analogies with Eastern Asia derive considerable support from those of a *physical nature.* The Aborigines of the Western World were distinguished by certain peculiarities of organization, which have led physiologists to regard them as a separate race. These peculiarities are shown in their reddish complexion, approaching a cinnamon color; their straight, black, and exceedingly glossy hair; their beard thin, and usually eradicated; their high cheek-bones, eyes obliquely directed towards the temples, prominent noses, and narrow foreheads falling backwards with a greater inclination than those of any other race except the African. From this general standard, however, there are deviations, in the same manner, if not to the same extent, as in other quarters of the globe, though these deviations do not seem to be influenced by the same laws of local position. Anatomists, also, have discerned in crania disinterred from the mounds, and in those inhabitants of the high plains of the Cordilleras, an obvious difference from those of the more barbarous tribes. This is seen especially in the ampler forehead, intimating a decided intellectual superiority. These characteristics are found to bear a close resemblance to those of the Mongolian family, and especially to the people of Eastern Tartary; so that, notwithstanding certain differences recognised by physiologists, the skulls of the two races could not be readily distinguished from one another by a common observer. No inference can be surely drawn, however, without a wide range of comparison. That hitherto made has been chiefly founded on specimens from the barbarous tribes. Perhaps a closer comparison with the more civilized may supply still stronger evidence of affinity.

In seeking for analogies with the Old World, we should not pass by in silence the *architectural remains* of the country, which, indeed, from their resemblance to the pyramidal structures of the East, have suggested to more than one antiquary the idea of a common origin. The Spanish invaders, it is true, assailed the Indian buildings, especially those of a religious character, with all the fury of fanaticism. The same spirit survived in the generations which succeeded. The war has never ceased against the monuments of the country; and the few that fanaticism has spared have been nearly all demolished to serve the purposes of utility. Of all the stately edifices, so much extolled by the Spaniards who first visited the country, there are scarcely more vestiges at the present day than are to be found in some of those regions of Europe and Asia, which once swarmed with populous cities, the great marts of luxury and commerce. Yet some of these remains, like the temple of Xochicalco, the palaces of

Tezcotzinco, the colossal calendar-stone in the capital, are of sufficient magnitude, and wrought with sufficient skill, to attest mechanical powers in the Aztecs not unworthy to be compared with those of the ancient Egyptians.

But, if the remains on the Mexican soil are so scanty, they multiply as we descend the south-eastern slopes of the Cordilleras, traverse the rich Valley of Oaxaca, and penetrate the forests of Chiapa and Yucatan. In the midst of these lonely regions, we meet with the ruins, recently discovered, of several ancient cities, Mitla, Palenque, and Itzalana or Uxmal, which argue a higher civilization than any thing yet found on the American continent; and, although it was not the Mexicans who built these cities, yet as they are probably the work of cognate races, the present inquiry would be incomplete without some attempt to ascertain what light they can throw on the origin of the Indian, and consequently of the Aztec, civilization.

Few works of art have been found in the neighborhood of any of the ruins. Some of them, consisting of earthen or marble vases, fragments of statues, and the like, are fantastic, and even hideous; others show much grace and beauty of design, and are apparently well executed. It may seem extraordinary,

Soon the Spaniards will come. It is interesting to see how the Aztec artists represented them:
above, battle scene. Below: the Mexican warriors attack a troop of invaders entrenched in a building.

that no iron in the buildings themselves, nor iron tools, should have been discovered, considering that the materials used are chiefly granite, very hard, and carefully hewn and polished. Red copper chisels and axes have been picked up in the midst of large blocks of granite imperfectly cut, with fragments of pillars and architraves, in the quarries near Mitla. Tools of a similar kind have been discovered, also, in the quarries near Thebes, and the difficulty, nay, impossibility, of cutting such masses from the living rock, with any tools which we possess, except iron, has confirmed an ingenious writer in the supposition, that this metal must have been employed by the Egyptians, but that its tendency to decomposition, especially in a nitrous soil, has prevented any specimens of it from being preserved. Yet iron has been found, after the lapse of some thousands of years, in the remains of antiquity; and it is certain, that the Mexicans, down to the time of the Conquest, used only copper instruments, with an alloy of tin, and a siliceous powder, to cut the hardest stones and some of them of enormous dimensions. This fact, with the additional circumstance, that only similar tools have been found in Central America, strengthens the conclusion, that iron was neither known

there, nor in ancient Egypt.

But what are the nations of the Old Continent, whose style of architecture bears most resemblance to that of the remarkable monuments of Chiapa and Yucatan? The points of resemblance will, probably, be found neither numerous nor decisive. There is, indeed, some analogy both to the Egyptian and Asiatic style of architecture in the pyramidal, terrace-formed bases on which the buildings repose, resembling, also, the Toltec and Mexican *teocalli*. A similar care, also, is observed in the people of both hemispheres, to adjust the position of their buildings by the cardinal points. The walls in both are covered with figures and hieroglyphics, which, on the American, as on the Egyptian, may be designed, perhaps, to record the laws and historical annals of the nation. These figures, as well as the buildings themselves, are found to have been stained with various dyes, principally vermilion; a favorite color with the Egyptians, also, who painted their colossal statues and temples of granite. Notwithstanding these points of similarity, the Palenque architecture has little to remind us of the Egyptian, or of the Oriental. It is, indeed, more conformable, in the perpendicular elevation of the walls, the moderate size of the stones, and the general arrangement of the parts, to the European. It must be admitted, however, to have a character of originality peculiar to itself.

More positive proofs of communication with the East might be looked for in their sculpture, and in the conventional forms of their hieroglyphics. But the sculptures on the Palenque buildings are in relief, unlike the Egyptian, which are usually in *intaglio*. The Egyptians were not very successful in their representations of the human figure, which are on the same invariable model, always in profile, from the greater facility of execution this presents over the front view; the full eye is placed on the side of the head, while the countenance is similar in all, and perfectly destitute of expression. The Palenque artists were equally awkward in representing the various attitudes of the body, which they delineated also in profile. But the parts are executed with much correctness, and sometimes gracefully; the costume is rich and various; and the ornamented head-dress, typical, perhaps, like the Aztec, of the name and condition of the party, conforms in its magnificence to the Oriental taste. The countenance is various, and often expressive. The contour of the head is, indeed, most extraordi-

nary, describing almost a semicircle from the forehead to the tip of the nose, and contracted towards the crown, whether from the artificial pressure practised by many of the Aborigines, or from some preposterous notion of ideal beauty. But, while superior in the execution of the details, the Palenque artist was far inferior to the Egyptian in the number and variety of the objects displayed by him, which, on the Theban temples, comprehend animals as well as men, and almost every conceivable object of use, or elegant art.

The hieroglyphics are too few on the American buildings to authorize any decisive inference. On comparing them, however, with those of the Dresden Codex, probably from this same quarter of the country, with those on the monument of Xochicalco, and with the ruder picture-writing of the Aztecs, it is not easy to discern any thing which indicates a common system. Still less obvious is the resemblance to the Egyptian characters, whose refined and delicate abbreviations approach almost to the simplicity of an alphabet. Yet the Palenque writing shows an advanced stage of the art; and, though somewhat clumsy, intimates, by the conventional and arbitrary forms of the hieroglyphics, that it was symbolical, and perhaps phonetic,

yepolính̄q mexica

in its character. That its mysterious import will ever be deciphered is scarcely to be expected. The language of the race who employed it, the race itself, is unknown. And it is not likely that another Rosetta stone will be found, with its trilingual inscription, to supply the means of comparison, and to guide the American Champollion in the path of discovery.

It is impossible to contemplate these mysterious monuments of a lost civilization, without a strong feeling of curiosity as to who were their architects, and what is their probable age. The data, on which to rest our conjectures of their age, are not very substantial; although some find in them a warrant for an antiquity of thousands of years, coeval with the architecture of Egypt and Hindostan. But the interpretation of hieroglyphics, and the apparent duration of trees, are vague and unsatisfactory. And how far can we derive an argument from the discoloration and dilapidated condition of the ruins, when we find so many structures of the Middle Ages dark and mouldering with decay, while the marbles of the Acropolis, and the grey stone of Pæstum, still shine in their primitive splendor?

There are, however, undoubted proofs of considerable age to be found there. Trees

have shot up in the midst of the buildings, which measure, it is said, more than nine feet in diameter. A still more striking fact is the accumulation of vegetable mould in one of the courts, to the depth of nine feet above the pavement. This in our latitude would be decisive of a very great antiquity. But, in the rich soil of Yucatan, and under the ardent sun of the tropics, vegetation bursts forth with irrepressible exuberance, and generations of plants succeed each other without intermission, leaving an accumulation of deposits, that would have perished under a northern winter. Another evidence of their age is afforded by the circumstance, that, in one of the courts of Uxmal, the granite pavement, on which the figures of tortoises were raised in relief, is worn nearly smooth by the feet of the crowds who have passed over it; a curious fact, suggesting inferences both in regard to the age and population of the place. Lastly, we have authority for carrying back the date of many of these ruins to a certain period, since they were found in a deserted, and probably dilapidated, state by the first Spaniards who entered the country. Their notices, indeed, are brief and casual, for the old Conquerors had little respect for works of art; and it is fortunate for these structures,

The Aztecs in front of the Spaniards (continued): Cortes received by the chiefs of Haxcala. Natives surrendering to Cortes.

that they had ceased to be the living temples of the gods, since no merit of architecture, probably, would have availed to save them from the general doom of the monuments of Mexico.

If we find it so difficult to settle the age of these buildings, what can we hope to know of their architects? Little can be gleaned from the rude people by whom they are surrounded. The old Tezcucan chronicler, so often quoted by me, the best authority for the traditions of his country, reports, that the Toltecs, on the breaking up of their empire,—which he places, earlier than most authorities, in the middle of the tenth century,—migrating from Anahuac, spread themselves over Guatemala, Tecuantepec, Campeachy, and the coasts and neighboring isles on both sides of the Isthmus. This assertion, important, considering its source, is confirmed by the fact, that several of the nations in that quarter adopted systems of astronomy and chronology, as well as sacerdotal institutions, very similar to the Aztec, which, as we have seen, were also probably derived from the Toltecs, their more polished predecessors in the land.

If so recent a date for the construction of the American buildings be thought incompatible with this oblivion of their origin, it should be remembered how treacherous a thing is tradition, and how easily the links of the chain are severed. The builders of the pyramids had been forgotten before the time of the earliest Greek historians. The antiquary still disputes, whether the frightful inclination of that architectural miracle, the tower of Pisa, standing, as it does, in the heart of a populous city, was the work of accident or design. And we have seen how soon the Tezcucans, dwelling amidst the ruins of their royal palaces, built just before the Conquest, had forgotten their history, while the more inquisitive traveller refers their construction to some remote period before the Aztecs.

The reader has now seen the principal points of coincidence insisted on between the civilization of ancient Mexico, and the eastern hemisphere. In presenting them to him, I have endeavored to confine myself to such as rest on sure historic grounds; and not so much to offer my own opinion, as to enable him to form one for himself. There are some material embarrassments in the way to this, however, which must not be passed over in silence. These consist, not in explaining the fact, that, while the mythic system and the science of the Aztecs afford some striking points of analogy with the Asiatic, they should differ in so many more; for the same phenomenon is found among the nations of the Old World, who seem to have borrowed from one another those ideas, only, best suited to their peculiar genius and institutions. Nor does the difficulty lie in accounting for the great dissimilarity of the American languages to those in the other hemisphere; for the difference with these is not greater than what exists among themselves; and no one will contend for a separate origin for each of the Aboriginal tribes. But it is scarcely possible to reconcile the knowledge of Oriental science with the total ignorance of some of the most serviceable and familiar arts, as the use of milk, and iron, for example; arts so simple, yet so important to domestic comfort, that, when once acquired, they could hardly be lost.

The Aztecs had no useful domesticated animals. And we have seen that they employed bronze, as a substitute for iron, for all mechanical purposes. The bison, or wild cow of America, however, which ranges in countless herds over the magnificent prairies of the west, yields milk like the tame animal of the same species, in Asia and Europe; and iron was scattered in large masses over the surface of the table-land. Yet there have been people considerably civilized in Eastern Asia, who were almost equally strangers to the use of milk. The buffalo range was not so much on the western coast, as on the eastern slopes of the Rocky Mountains; and the migratory Aztec might well doubt, whether the wild, uncouth monsters, whom he occasionally saw bounding with such fury over the distant plains, were capable of domestication, like the meek animals which he had left grazing in the green pastures of Asia. Iron, too, though met with on the surface of the ground, was more tenacious, and harder to work, than copper, which he also found in much greater quantities on his route. It is possible, moreover, that his migration may have been previous to the time when iron was used by his nation; for we have seen more than one people in the Old World employing bronze and copper, with entire ignorance, apparently, of any more serviceable metal.—Such is the explanation, unsatisfactory, indeed, but the best that suggests itself, of this curious anomaly.

The consideration of these and similar difficulties has led some writers to regard the antique American civilization as purely indigenous. Whichever way we turn, the subject is full of embarrassment. It is easy, indeed, by fastening the attention on one portion of it, to come to a conclusion. In this

153

way, while some feel little hesitation in pro-
nouncing the American civilization original;
others, no less certainly, discern in it a
Hebrew, or an Egyptian, or a Chinese, or a
Tartar origin, as their eyes are attracted by
the light of analogy too exclusively to this or
the other quarter. The number of contra-
dictory lights, of itself, perplexes the judgment,
and prevents us from arriving at a precise
and positive inference. Indeed, the affectation
of this, in so doubtful a matter, argues a most
unphilosophical mind. Yet, where there is
most doubt, there is often the most dogma-
tism.

The reader of the preceding pages may,
perhaps, acquiesce in the general conclusions,
—not startling by their novelty,—

First, that the coincidences are sufficiently
strong to authorize a belief, that the civilization
of Anahuac was, in some degree, influenced
by that of Eastern Asia.

And, secondly, that the discrepancies are
such as to carry back the communication to a
very remote period; so remote, that this
foreign influence has been too feeble to inter-
fere materially with the growth of what may
be regarded, in its essential features, as a
peculiar and indigenous civilization.

Index

Printed in Italy